Ul
E

The *Ultimate Guide to Business Writing* is a comprehensive guide on how to write any kind of business document. Written clearly in an engaging voice, it explains in depth the whole process: from determining objectives to establishing readers' needs, conducting research, outlining, and designing a template; to writing the first draft; to editing for meaning, accuracy, concision, style and emotional impact; to creating glossaries and indices; to proofreading and working with reviewers.

The book also explains how to exploit the psychology of perception and motivation, collaborate effectively with business colleagues, manage documents holistically across an organisation, and deal with the other everyday practicalities of managing knowledge in a corporate environment. Every section of the book is packed with questions to stimulate thinking and generate meaningful answers, and dozens of examples of what works and why. The book's also rich in practical examples drawn from real life, anecdotes, humour, and visual aids. But the advice isn't just practical and anecdotal: it's also rigorously supported by scientific evidence from notable linguists and psychologists such as Steven Pinker, Daniel Goleman and Yellowlees Douglas. And anyone keen to explore further will benefit from the bibliography and links to videos and other online resources.

The book is ideal not just for professional business writers, such as editors, technical writers, copywriters and creative directors; it's also suitable for anyone whose job requires them to write, whether it's something as simple as an email or as complex as a set of policies or a handbook.

Julian Maynard-Smith is a business writer and knowledge manager with over 30 years of experience, principally in financial services and IT. He's worked in the UK, France and Germany, and runs his own company providing consultancy, training and coaching.

ULTIMATE GUIDE TO BUSINESS WRITING

ALL THE SECRETS OF CREATING AND MANAGING BUSINESS DOCUMENTS

Julian Maynard-Smith

Routledge
Taylor & Francis Group
LONDON AND NEW YORK

First published 2021
by Routledge
2 Park Square, Milton Park, Abingdon, Oxon OX14 4RN

and by Routledge
52 Vanderbilt Avenue, New York, NY 10017

Routledge is an imprint of the Taylor & Francis Group, an informa business

British Library Cataloguing-in-Publication Data
A catalogue record for this book is available from the British Library

Library of Congress Cataloging-in-Publication Data
Names: Maynard-Smith, Julian, 1964– author.
Title: The ultimate guide to business writing: discover all the secrets of creating and managing business documents / Julian Maynard-Smith.
Description: First Edition. | New York: Routledge, 2021. |
Includes bibliographical references and index. | Identifiers: LCCN 2020041505 (print) |
LCCN 2020041506 (ebook) | ISBN 9780367700188 (hardback) |
ISBN 9780367700195 (paperback) | ISBN 9781003144250 (ebook)
Subjects: LCSH: Business writing.
Classification: LCC HF5718.3 .M39 2021 (print) | LCC HF5718.3 (ebook) |
DDC 808.06/668—dc23
LC record available at https://lccn.loc.gov/2020041505
LC ebook record available at https://lccn.loc.gov/2020041506

ISBN: 978-0-367-70018-8 (hbk)
ISBN: 978-0-367-70019-5 (pbk)
ISBN: 978-1-003-14425-0 (ebk)

Typeset in Bembo
by codeMantra

MIX
Paper from responsible sources
FSC
www.fsc.org
FSC™ C013985

Printed in the United Kingdom
by Henry Ling Limited

CONTENTS

PREFACE

If you have any kind of office job, especially in a heavily regulated industry such as finance or the public sector, the amount of documentation you're expected to write is staggering: not just emails but also policies, procedures, user guides, monthly reports, business plans, white papers, case studies, and more. Increasing competitiveness, the global economy, complex regulation, all of these factors mean that being able to write well is no longer a luxury: it's a necessity.

This book shows you how to write any kind of business document logically, clearly and persuasively, even if you consider yourself poor at writing. Forget the myth you need some kind of gift to write well: writing's a mixture of artistry and carpentry, and this book gives you all the tools you need to build solid documents with seamless joinery and plenty of polish.

I've spent over thirty years helping people like you, meaning what you're about to learn isn't just theory but hard-won experience of what works and why; and what's taken me decades to discover you can learn in minutes. Before you know it you'll be writing with more clarity, more style and more confidence. And you'll see amazing results too, both personal and professional.

ABOUT THE AUTHOR

My name's Julian Maynard-Smith and I've crafted words (as a technical author, documentation manager, copywriter, editor, proofreader and translator) since 1989, in the UK, France and Germany, working for software companies, banks and insurers. I'm also a music journalist, and write crime fiction under a pseudonym.

www.betterbusinesswriting.info

1

HOW TO WRITE ANY DOCUMENT

You're about to discover all the steps for creating any business document. The steps are organised to guide you as efficiently as possible from conception to completion, so you're best off following them in order – at least to start with. You can always dip in and out for help in specific areas once you're familiar with the process.

With that in mind, let's crack on with the first step.

CONSIDER WHAT OUTCOMES YOU WANT

Every business document needs to achieve an outcome, or what's the point of writing it? You write a policy to get colleagues to do good stuff (and stop doing bad stuff); marketing material to persuade buyers to buy from you, not your competitors; functional specs so that the tech guys know what to build. And so on.

So before you even think of writing anything, be it an email or a 200-page manual, here's what you need to work out first:

1 What outcomes do I want?
2 Who's my audience?
3 *Why should they care?*

Consider the person who asked for my help with a document and answered these questions with, 'Dunno. My manager just asked me to write it.' How would you rate that document's chances of achieving its desired outcomes? Writing without knowing your outcomes and audience is like driving without a destination, eyes squeezed shut and deaf to the shouts from your passengers.

Once you're clear on your outcomes (your destination), your satnav for *everything* is your readers: who they are, where they want to be taken, and why they'd want to journey with you. This is true even for that most all-about-me genre of books, autobiographies, because autobiographies that don't appeal to their readers simply won't get read. And, as a Chinese proverb puts it, an unread book is just a pile of paper.

It's a point I'll bang on and on and on about throughout this book: *why should your readers care*? And how can you show them you care?

By finding out who they are and what they want.

So let's look at that next.

RESEARCH YOUR READERS

The only two reasons people read anything are because they need to or because they want to. And even when they need to they often won't, if it's a chore to do so. Think of those terms and conditions so boring we click 'Accept' without reading them: for all we know, we've unwittingly agreed to sell Google or Amazon our kidneys.

Our job as writers, then, is to understand what our readers need and want. And what's the best way to do that? Ask them – and listen. The book *Mindwise*, by psychologist Nicholas Epley, gives plenty of compelling evidence that people wildly overestimate their skill at knowing others, even their spouses. In short, if you guess what people are thinking you're likely to be wrong. You need to ask and verify.

Talk to your readers

When communicating with readers, ask yourself the following questions.

Am I hearing my readers' needs first-hand?

Unless you communicate directly with your readers, be they internal or external, it's easy to misconstrue or lose sight of their needs: especially when intermediaries with their own agendas get in the way, such as project managers pushing hard to meet delivery dates, account managers chasing revenue, or department heads wanting to cut costs.

Best of all are face-to-face discussions with your readers. If your readers are colleagues in the same office, go and talk to them rather than emailing them. If they're colleagues in another office or external people try to meet them anyway, eg through site visits, training courses and seminars. Other options include user groups, surveys, questionnaires and suchlike: you can run an online survey quite easily using a web tool such as www.surveymonkey.com or www.smartsurvey.co.uk.

Am I communicating regularly?

It's important to stay on track by asking questions such as 'Does it cover everything you need?' and 'Is this the right level of depth for you?' and 'Is there anything you find confusing?' Avoid asking vague questions such as 'Do you like it?' or 'Does it look OK?' because you risk distractions such as people bickering over the font or your writing style. The main thing at this stage is to ensure that readers 'get' the content and that it meets their needs. And if it's a document that requires approval, you're much more likely to get sign-off first time round if you've engaged your audience throughout.

Regular engagement also protects you as the writer. I know freelance writers who've been denied payment by unscrupulous clients claiming they didn't follow the brief, and it's harder for a client to rip you off if you have an audit trail to prove you delivered exactly what they asked for.

When do people need this information?

Most people when having to write a document think to ask, 'When does it need to be finished?' But a smarter question is, 'Who needs what by when?' That way you can apply triage if time's short. For example:

- Different people may need the same information at different times. Say you're writing a functional spec for new software: it makes sense to ensure that the design team get their information before the developers get theirs, since design comes before development.
- Or maybe the same readers need some information now and the rest later, in which case you can concentrate on perfecting the 'now' information and ignore the 'later' information for a later release.
- Or maybe your readers need to get the big picture right now but aren't too fussed about the details, in which case you can give them a draft then continue editing while they're reviewing the draft.

Whatever the scenario, if you're pressed for time the order of the steps in this guide will help you, as early steps (eg designing the structure and clarifying your meaning) are more fundamental than the later ones (eg trimming words).

Finally, always allow more time for delivering a document than you think you need. Why? Well, first you need to allow for contingencies such as holidays, uncooperative or tardy colleagues, and people being moved to other projects. Second, there's often a long chain of dependencies between writing and delivery, such as getting documents reviewed and approved.

It's especially important to plan well for documents with hard deadlines such as submissions to a regulator or bid responses to a prospect. In such cases, it's wise to plan dates backwards. For example, 'If the regulator is to get the document by 30 November, the printers need at least a day, which means it needs to be signed off by the board no later than 28 November, and allowing a week for board review means the executive committee needs the document by 21 November …'. And so on.

Which media do readers prefer?

Ask your audience how they want the information presented. For example, there's often an automatic assumption that board members want PowerPoint decks, but decks are usually a bad choice for anything other than animated slideshows (something we'll examine in more detail later).

Consider other media beyond Microsoft Word v PowerPoint, such as your company's intranet, a wiki or training videos, or even a blend of media. For this guide I'm assuming you're writing a document, but always bear in mind that other options are available and may be better.

Have I instilled trust and openness?

Have you ever seen the TV series *Undercover Boss*? The premise is simple: a senior executive is disguised and takes a low-level job in their own firm. It's only then, once they've gained the trust of their employees, that they discover what their employees really think, feel or even *do*. You need to build a similar level of trust: particularly if you're senior or your role could be perceived as policing (such as internal audit); or if people feel threatened, eg if your company's planning layoffs. Otherwise, people are likely to tell you what you want to hear – or stonewall you.

For example, I once did a contract where the boss announced that several job roles would be offshored, and simultaneously expected people to start sharing more information about what they did. And guess what? Everyone clammed up.

Understand your readers' needs

To understand your readers' needs, ask yourself the following questions.

What do readers want or have to do?

Do your readers need to operate something (user guide), understand how something works (functional specification), learn what rules to follow (policy), form a judgement or determine actions to take based on advice (report), discover the benefits of a product or service (white paper), or something else?

Understanding needs helps you structure your information, eg reports are focused on findings and advice ('What were the results and what actions are needed?'), user guides are focused on tasks ('How do I?'), specifications on functions ('What's this for?'), and white papers on reasons ('Why buy this product or service?').

Fail to establish needs and you risk producing a document that's useless. For example, a policy's purpose is simple: to tell people what they must (and must not) do. Yet many times I've edited policies riddled with statements such as 'Monitoring is performed regularly' that fail to address the fundamental question, '*Who* has to do this?'

And discovering what your readers *do* is far more enlightening than guessing from what they're *called*. When a former colleague of mine was asked to write a report for 'ExCo' he naturally assumed his readers were the executive committee. Too late he discovered it was the board so his report failed. Had he asked what they did or needed to achieve, the problem would never have arisen.

What's the most suitable tone of voice?

Different objectives need different tones of voice, what in literary parlance is called 'register'. For example, a sales agreement for a client will probably need a more formal, sober register than text for colleagues. Similarly, the emphatic tone needed for a policy ('You must') would be alienating in a guidebook, where readers expect not a sergeant-major barking orders but a friendly guide saying things such as 'Let's look at …' and 'A good tip is …'.

Also consider emotional state. For instance, people reading instructions on how to get a refund are likely to be frustrated and annoyed (so apologise), readers of a sales message might be sceptical (so reassure them), and readers of a policy might be bored (so get to the point). Similarly, consider power dynamics: deferential (but not fawning) to someone higher up, assertive yet supportive (*not* bullying) to someone lower down.

And what about factors such as age, gender, nationality and ethnicity? Are your readers typically men or women? Baby-boomers or millennials? Any cultural sensitivities you need to heed? All such factors can affect the tone of voice you adopt.

With so much affecting tone of voice, is there a simple way to determine the best tone? Yes, there is. If you're writing to a specific person and you have a sample of their own writing (perhaps you're responding to an email) a surprisingly simple and clever trick to get the tone right is to mirror their word choices. Like mirroring someone's body language, it's a great way to build an emotional bond (so long as you don't overdo it).

And if you're writing for a group of people, check out what they're likely to enjoy reading and mirror that. Books, magazines and newspapers are great because they're pitched at clearly delineated markets, and their tone varies accordingly. Readers of the *Economist* expect a different tone from readers of *Hello!* magazine. Similarly, a retired woman whose favourite magazines are *Homes & Gardens* and *The Lady* is unlikely to be won over by the bro talk in *Muscle & Fitness* (although, who knows, she might like the photos).

The best publications for you to read are books written by leaders in your profession, serious business journals, and trade magazines. One thing you will notice when you read them is that serious does *not* mean stuffy or pompous – even so-called 'serious' periodicals are nowadays written in a direct and conversational tone.

Tone of voice is hugely important so later on, when we explore how to edit effectively, we'll look at it in greater depth. For now, just bear in mind that your tone of voice needs to suit your readers' objectives.

Do several types of reader need this information?

Often, one document can be successfully aimed at several types of readers, eg an underwriting guide that has an executive overview for board members and more detailed chapters aimed at actuaries and underwriters. Combining information into as few documents as possible helps to reduce the maintenance burden and minimises duplication.

Which aspects of the topic matter to my readers?

What's important to your audience? What are they trying to achieve? Car manuals for mechanics are totally different from those for drivers, even if the car model is the same. Similarly, if you're writing a guide to an e-trading application, IT administrators are mainly concerned with the system's architecture but may be marginally interested in how to enter trades; traders don't care about anything beneath the interface; and the IT support team probably need to understand both the technology and the interface.

Decide how much to explain

Now you understand your readers' objectives, you need to decide how much to explain. Ask yourself the following questions.

Do I explain what readers might know already?

Readers would rather be patronised than confused or misled, so if in doubt err towards over-explaining. On this point it's worth considering something called Grice's maxim of quantity, named after a British philosopher of language called Paul Grice, which states that we should be *as informative as required* (but no more).

The best way to understand this maxim is to see what happens when it's violated, so here's an example. Suppose you ask someone for directions to the nearest pharmacy. If that person knows where it is but also that it's closed for lunch, they've violated the maxim if they give you directions without warning you it won't be open till two. Another example is a scene in the movie *The Pink Panther Strikes Again* when the bumbling Inspector Clouseau asks a hotel owner if his dog bites and is then bitten when he tries to stroke it: 'I thought you said your dog doesn't bite,' says Clouseau. 'That,' replies the hotel owner, 'is not my dog.'

In other words, as writers we often have a duty to *anticipate* reader needs – hence why it's always wise to err on the side of over-explaining.

Another principle worth recalling on this point is one from the world of design. It's called 'forgiveness' and it means always making it easy for people to get out of trouble, a classic example being the Esc button on a computer keyboard.

If you're worried about annoying more knowledgeable readers by over-explaining, you can always help them skip to what's relevant to them with cues such as, 'If you're already familiar with the basics, you can skip to chapter 3' or 'You need to read this chapter only if you're a system administrator.' And if information is of only secondary importance to all readers, either put it in an appendix or (often better) give a link to an external source.

Can I progress from basics to details?

We've seen how progressing from basics to details is a great way to address the needs of both novices and more knowledgeable readers. But it works a treat whatever the knowledge levels of your readers, especially in materials designed to teach. It's called the 'spiral approach' and it works like this: explain something basic, introduce details and relate those details to the basics so readers can assimilate them, build on the newly integrated details to introduce more details, and so on. Think of spirals in nature: seashells, animal horns, the Milky Way. The spiral approach to learning is the same idea: grow by building outwards from a solid foundation.

In fact, the technique of progressing from known to unknown is so effective it has various other names, including progressive disclosure and the given-new principle. We're jumping slightly ahead of ourselves, because later on we examine the most effective ways to structure content, of which given-new is just one. For now, just remember that over-explaining need never be a problem, because by structuring your information effectively you can always keep the level of detail just right.

What depth of detail does my audience care about?

Consider a report on the activities of a committee within a single business unit: the committee itself expects a lot of detail, the BU's board is probably happy with a summary, and the group board probably doesn't want the report at all.

Are my readers specialists or not?

Whenever you're writing for general readers, choose everyday words over jargon. For example, a heart surgeon would use the phrase 'myocardial infarction' if writing a peer-reviewed paper for the *Lancet* but 'heart attack' if writing a health leaflet for the public.

Readers interpret text in the way that makes most sense from their viewpoint, not the writer's. For this reason, you need to be especially careful with ordinary-sounding words with specialist meanings. To a surgeon a 'ligature' is a suture, to a saxophonist it's the thing that clamps a reed to a mouthpiece, to a typographer it's what joins two letters into a single shape – and to a coroner it's what killed the victim.

Similarly, remember that abbreviations can stand for more than one thing and that people will default to whichever meaning is most familiar to them. Take 'PDF', which is most likely to mean 'probability distribution forecast' to an actuary but 'portable document format' to almost everyone else. Or 'CMS', which most people will interpret as being a management system of some sort: but what on earth does the 'C' stand for? For marketing professionals it's *customer*, for complaints handlers it's *complaints*, and for technical authors it's *content* (and in my time I've seen all three).

And how about this abbreviation, from an insurance company's internal policy I edited? '£250,000 GWP' – I misinterpreted 'GWP' as a typo for 'GBP' (British pounds sterling) and 'corrected' it. It turned out the original was right, standing for 'gross written premium'. So, two lessons in one: authors should spell out abbreviations; and even seasoned editors should check with the author when in any doubt about the writer's intentions. With the final draft amended to '£250,000 gross written premium (GWP)' no one's likely to get confused.

What's the relationship between readers and us?

Is the audience internal? External? If external, are they clients, prospects, third-party vendors, business partners, financial regulators, someone else? The answer to this question can trigger further questions such as:

- If the audience is internal, are there any politics or turf wars to bear in mind? For example, if you're implementing group-wide change, do any business units feel resentful because they feel that HQ's telling them how to run their business (meaning you may need to adopt a conciliatory tone or get them more involved)? Or if you're in an audit department, do your reports need to be forceful without being antagonistic (which again needs diplomatic language)?

- If you're writing for third-party suppliers, is there any insider knowledge to explain? For example, company jargon and abbreviations, and 'how we do things round here'?
- If you're producing a report for clients, how glossy do they expect it to be? For example, are they prepared to pay extra for sophisticated graphic design and professional typesetting, or would a relatively unadorned Word/PDF document suffice? Any cross-client sensitivities you need to consider? Any confidentiality issues?

Are my readers native speakers?

Especially for international readers, avoid slang, idioms and obscure words. Basic English, a limited vocabulary often used to teach those starting English as a second language, consists of only 850 basic words and their permutations (eg past participles), so even complex ideas require few words. In fact, only about 100 words account for nearly 50% of everything said and written in English.

If this last fact surprises you, consider that word frequencies obey Zipf's law, meaning that the commonest word in any language occurs roughly twice as often as the second commonest, three times as often as the third commonest, and so on.

Also be aware that even if your readers have English as their mother tongue, they will warm more to your text if you consider regional variations. For example, if your London office is writing a proposal for a US client, it's better to use US English.

If you think US/UK English isn't a big deal, consider the localisation industry, which specialises in customising products and services to specific countries or regions – it even has people who call themselves '*UK to US translators*'. Or consider a seemingly trivial matter such as punctuation: in the UK and United States, '5,000' means 'five thousand' but in French and other languages it means 'five to three decimal points' because the use of full stops and commas in numbers is reversed.

Another regional variation to remember is time. If you're referring to times and some or all of your readers are in another time zone, make sure you clarify which time zone you're referring to, eg 'The meeting will be at 14:00 (UTC).' As a further courtesy you can give the time in their time zone or, for maximum clarity, specify both: '14:00 (UTC) / 09:00 (EST).'

Similarly, for dates it's best to supply the month as a word rather than numeral to avoid confusion between DD-MM-YY (as used in the UK) and MM-DD-YY (as used in the United States). Note too that the UK format has no comma (4 July 2020) whereas the US format takes a comma after the day (July 4, 2020).

GATHER YOUR INFORMATION

Now you need to gather your information. The better prepared you are before writing, the easier your job will be.

Check what's available and where

For much of your material you may need to rely on primary sources (your direct knowledge, interviews with experts, surveys, test data, and so on) but secondary sources (articles, existing company documents, meeting minutes, etc) can be very helpful too – and save you a lot of time.

Let's look at what to check.

Is this information documented already?

Check whether anything you're proposing to write is already documented. This simple check can save you from having to 'rewrite the wheel' because you can simply cross-refer to the existing material rather than having to create it yourself. Let's call this the 'outsourcing principle'.

The information source can either be internal (eg a page on your company intranet) or external (eg Wikipedia for general knowledge, a vendor's website for descriptions of a third-party product, or a professional association's website for a glossary of industry-specific terms). So check other information sources, both internal and external, and ask around.

Suggesting you check if information exists already might sound like stating the obvious. But you'd be surprised by how often people waste time duplicating perfectly serviceable information available in the public domain. Someone once asked me to help fix the formatting for a questionnaire he'd obviously struggled with for quite some time. I sorted it out for him. Next question? 'Can you now help me put the regulator's *new* text into the questionnaire?' Meaning he'd wasted time rebranding a regulator's standard questionnaire to look like the company's – then wasted *my* time faffing around untangling his formatting. And the reason he was rebranding the questionnaire in the first place was to change it from the template of an earlier company acquired by his. Meaning that at least three people had wasted their time on reformatting, for no gain whatsoever.

Another reason that external links are better than copying and pasting is that you remove the risk of your version going out of date when the source changes; and (for third-party material) you remove any risk of plagiarism. The only downside is that you have no control over whether the source material is kept up to date, deleted or moved: so if you do link to external sources, make sure those sources are reliable and periodically check that the links still work.

Can this information be generated?

Check whether the information you want to document can be auto-generated by the software you're using. This is often the case with spreadsheets, databases and other software designed for manipulating lists, statistics, charts and suchlike. I've often seen people waste time typing tabular data by hand, even drawing graphics by hand, when they could have generated them instead. This usually happens when people are misusing PowerPoint to produce 'decks', namely documents by another name. (Using PowerPoint for anything other than slideshows is a frequent and pervasive waste of time. More on this later.)

Decide whether to update, clone or create

If you need to produce a document that's similar to an existing one, you have three options: update, clone then adapt, or create from scratch. To decide which option is best, ask yourself the following questions.

Is the existing document in good shape? (If not, create from scratch)

Documents are worth updating if they're already in good shape. If they're too badly written or formatted to salvage, you're usually better off creating a new document and treating the existing one like a mechanic treats a wrecked car: only good for scavenging spare parts. Later you'll discover how to structure a document; and it's relatively easy to lift spare parts from a bad document into a well-structured one.

If you've created a new document from a 'wrecked car', ideally your new document will completely replace the old. If for whatever reason you need to keep the old one, make sure you update it to show it's been replaced and provide a URL to where the new document is stored.

Warning: If you're using Microsoft Word and pasting text from a messy document into a clean one, it's wise to paste *unformatted* text to avoid inheriting formatting gremlins. By default, Word pastes with formatting but you can select 'text only' instead or set 'text only' as the default paste option. Word's help explains how.

How similar are the source and target documents? (If cloning, be careful)

The more similar a document is to the one you need to produce, the stronger the argument for updating or cloning, rather than creating from scratch. For instance, suppose you have a policy that needs refreshing each year – it's tempting create a copy then adapt it to what's new for this year. Before you do, though, ask yourself:

- Is the existing document in good shape (see above)? If the existing policy is a mess, consider creating a new document from scratch rather than trying to unmangle the old one. Documents updated year after year often deteriorate, and sometimes they reach a point of no return and it's best to start afresh.
- Is any of the content sensitive or potentially embarrassing? For example, suppose you're considering cloning a Client-X document for Client-Y and can't risk leaving any trace of the other client.

  If you're using Microsoft Word, cloning client-sensitive documents is highly risky. If you must do it (and I don't recommend it – using a template is safer) remember not only to do a 'find and replace' throughout the whole document but also to check the document's properties, since fields such as Author, Title and Subject can contain inherited (and embarrassingly revealing) information. Such as the fact that the author ripped off the document from the last place they worked. Don't snigger – I've seen it happen.

Assess your information sources

Before relying on any existing content, ask yourself the following questions.

Is this information up to date and relevant?

Sometimes people, in their desire to be 'helpful', will give you any old information for 'background' or as 'examples' – if you take the material on faith, you'll waste a lot of time reworking irrelevant or superseded material (as I've done myself).

Therefore, it's always wise to ask the authors why they're giving you this information and how reliable it is. And doing so offers further advantages: people often explain things better when talking than when writing, and you get instant replies to your initial questions and further clarifications.

Can I find clues to what confuses people?

Look for problems and complaints occurring repeatedly in emails, phone calls, error logs, meeting minutes and suchlike. Recurring problems can give clues as to where your documentation needs attention.

For example, if you work for a software company and one area of functionality is generating a suspiciously high number of change requests and bug reports, consider that it may not be the software that's at fault but user errors caused by faulty documentation.

Have I assessed all sources before ploughing ahead?

Have you heard the cautionary tale of examinees being asked to read the entire exam paper before answering any of the questions? Those who follow this simple instruction find an instruction towards the end that says, 'You can ignore all the other questions and answer only this one.'

A similar principle applies to source materials, in that if you do read ahead you get a much clearer idea of which material's worth your attention and which isn't: meaning you won't waste time reworking shoddy material before discovering the better material you should have been using all along.

Can I combine documents?

If the same or similar information is repeated across documents, combine the documents: it's better for readers (everything they need in the same place) and better for you (fewer documents to manage). A smart approach is to put any overlapping information, such as executive summaries, at the front of your new document and material unique to each document in the later chapters.

And here's an even more important reason for combining documents that share information: in accordance with Murphy's law ('anything that can go wrong will go wrong'), different versions of the same content will infallibly drift apart into multiple versions of the supposed 'truth'. Worse, the very things described in the documents may drift apart as well.

For example, suppose you're an insurance company with different lines of business or geographies priced using the same or similar models and processes. Great – you've got standardisation and consistency, and all the business benefits that follow.

But what happens if you create separate documents per business line or geography (or, worse, both)? People will inevitably start perceiving those markets as different and your once-standardised pricing will start getting encrusted with differences, especially if the documents are owned by different people or stored in different places. And before you know it you'll be saddled with different tools, different processes, different everything. And that drift could in turn lead to more severe problems such as mispricing, missed opportunities, customer complaints and even the unwelcome attention of your regulators.

For similar reasons, always resist the temptation to copy-paste text. For example, a proposal doesn't need to regurgitate large chunks of the client's request for proposal (RFP), and regulatory submissions don't need to parrot the legislation text. Duplicating text is both time-consuming and risky. For instance, if a submission quotes legislation, what happens if the legislation changes and the author forgets (or doesn't know) the duplicated text needs updating? And what if a reader then takes those out-of-date regulations on trust and acts accordingly?

Consider information stability and longevity

Information that's in flux is hard to use, and its expected shelf life will affect how you structure your document. Ask yourself the following questions.

Am I trying to document information that's in flux?

Suppose you're writing a document that cross-refers to lots of associated documents. If the associated documents are still in flux (eg changing their names, still being written, or being split or combined) wait till they've settled down before adding all the cross-references. Trying to hit an ever-moving target, draft after draft, causes untold pain. Concentrate on what's stable.

Does all the information have a similar shelf life?

Suppose you're writing a report containing both strategic advice covering a five-year horizon and year-end results for the current year. If you document year-end results in the guide, you'll shorten the guide's shelf life – but the information's still important.

Your choices here include:

- Putting the volatile information where it's easy to replace, eg in an appendix.
- Putting the volatile information elsewhere: another document, intranet site, or wherever.

  To make it easy for readers to access the volatile information, you can simply add its URL within the more stable document. For example, within the strategy document covering a five-year horizon you can have a URL to the Results_2020 document. Next year, you simply update the URL to point to Results_2021 instead.

SELECT/ADAPT A TEMPLATE

Now you've gathered and assessed your information sources, you need to select a document template.

If your company has a standard Microsoft Word document template, resist the temptation to adapt it. That way you don't waste your time (and other people's) faffing around with formatting, and you ensure that your document adheres to your company's house style.

If you need to create a template, keep the formatting simple because the document's genes will be passed to other documents – so anything defective or elaborate, anything fiddly and irksome, will escalate into a major headache and timewaster. A well-designed template will remove the need for ad-hoc formatting, which always creates pain.

The following sections give you an idea of what to consider when designing a template in Word. For the specifics, check Word's online help.

Choose suitable typefaces (fonts)

First, some terminology: strictly speaking, Arial, Times New Roman, Garamond, etc are *typefaces*, a *font* being the typeface plus attributes such as size and weight (eg Arial 12-point italic v Arial 10-point bold). The terms are now largely interchangeable to all but specialists so for 'typeface' read 'font', if that's the term familiar to you.

When choosing typefaces, ask yourself the following questions.

Are the typefaces standard?

Unless you have a compelling reason for doing otherwise, such as a companywide house style, stick to standard typefaces. Why? Because if someone else opens a document and they don't have your nonstandard typeface installed, the document will be displayed with another – and this erodes your company's brand identity and can also mess up layouts because other typefaces occupy a different amount of space, even at the same point size.

How many typefaces do I actually need?

You rarely need more two typefaces, namely one for body text and (optionally) a contrasting typeface for headings. I say 'generally' because on rare occasions you may need more, such as to demarcate software code in an IT document – but such instances are relatively rare. Two typefaces are nearly always enough.

Which typefaces work best?

People read documents on both screen and paper, so it's wise to pick a typeface that works well for both. Some modern typefaces (like Georgia, Verdana, Cambria and Calibri) have been designed for maximum legibility online and they can work well on paper as well, so they're good choices.

Three significant factors to consider when selecting a typeface are serif / sans serif, x-height, and proportional / non-proportional. Before we go into the details, here are some examples – all shown at the same point size, which goes to show how much a typeface can affect a layout:

Serif (Times New Roman)

Sans serif (Arial)

Low x-height (Garamond)

High x-height (Georgia)

Proportional (Arial Narrow)

`Non-proportional (Courier)`

Figure 1.1 Typeface examples

Serifs are extra lines on the end of letter strokes – in the figure above, compare the capital S for 'Serif' (which is Times New Roman) with that for 'Sans serif' (Arial) and you'll see the difference. Generally, sans serif is best for headings and serif for body text – and using both provides an effective contrast. Also, an old rule of thumb stated that sans serif was best for screen and serif for print. This rule still holds to some extent, eg Times New Roman (serif) looks horrible on screen, and page after page of Arial (sans serif) can become wearisome on paper. But newer typefaces provide good exceptions to this rule. For example, the online versions of UK quality newspapers use serif typefaces that are highly legible, in part because they have a tall x-height: the height occupied by a lowercase x and, by extension, other letters of the same height, such as v, w and z. The taller the x-height in relation to ascenders (the bits of letters that stick above the x-line, as with b and l) and descenders (the bits that point down, as with g and y), the 'fatter' the typeface looks – and the more legible in relation to low-x-height typefaces when the text is small or the screen resolution low. In the figure above, notice how Georgia appears much more prominent than Garamond due to the difference in x-heights.

Proportional typefaces are ones where letter widths vary, eg a capital W is much wider than a capital I. With non-proportional typefaces every letter is the same width, eg a capital W is horizontally squashed to make it artificially narrow but a capital I has huge horizontal serifs to make it artificially wide. Non-proportional typefaces were originally designed to prevent typewriters from jamming and have largely been superseded by proportional typefaces. But one occasion on which they're extremely useful is when you need letters to align with each other vertically, as with software code.

Automate headers and footers

How can you make headers and footers low-maintenance for you but still richly informative for readers? Here's what I normally do:

- ✓ Avoid headers (or have something simple such as the company logo) and keep the footer as simple as possible.
- ✓ Centre-align any text and graphics, because doing so removes the risk of a portrait-width header/footer on a landscape section (or vice versa). It also removes the risk of a recto-verso layout looking weird if printed single-sided. Recto-verso layouts are where the front side of a page ('recto') and reverse side ('verso') differ, typically to make page numbers always appear on the outer edge of pages and to produce a visually appealing 'mirrored' effect across page spreads – an effect that's lost if a document's printed single-sided.
- ✓ Include the page count: in other words, rather than having *Page <n>* you have *Page <n> of <N>*, where *N* is the total number of pages. This way, readers can tell where any page is located in relation to the whole and, more importantly, which is the last page (something that's not always obvious).
- ✓ If using Word, add <filename> and <last saved> fields. This saves you from having to hand-type the document's name in the header/footer, and means that every page is automatically date/time-stamped with when the document was last saved – great for version control.

Keep styles simple

If you're using Microsoft Word, minimise the number of paragraph and character styles, and make sure that their formatting attributes are unfussy: no weird line spacing, borders, frames, and suchlike. Often, accepting Word's defaults is the safest course.

The problem with creating extra styles is that you confuse people and increase the chance they'll use the wrong ones, leading to mess and inconsistency. In particular, for heading styles stick to Word's defaults of Heading 1, Heading 2, etc – if you create heading styles based on anything else, the headings can't be used in cross-references and won't automatically appear in tables of contents.

It's also often wise to lock down formatting to prevent other authors from being 'creative' with a template, which you can do using Word's 'Restrict Editing' function.

Use ragged right margins

'Align left' (aka 'flush-left' or 'ragged-right') is usually preferable to 'justify' (ie spacing words to make each line the same width).

Why? Because justification:

- ✗ Creates word gaps that make text harder to read: up to 10% harder, according to some studies, and especially hard for people with dyslexia.
- ✗ Never looks as good in a Word document as it does in a professionally published book, because Word lacks the sophistication of typesetting software.
- ✗ Has a relentless blockiness, lacking the varying line lengths of a ragged margin that help to guide the eye from line to line.
- ✗ Often produces what in typography are called 'rivers', namely vertical gaps in a block of text caused by awkward word spacing.

For text in columns, justified text can improve legibility by giving a sharper definition to the gaps between columns, what are called 'alleys' (some people call them 'gutters' but, strictly speaking, the gutter is the blank space between margins on facing pages along with any extra space required for binding). In the trade-off between rivers and alleys, you may want to try both ragged and justified text to see which works best.

Create table styles

Most people know about Microsoft Word's paragraph and character styles, but did you know you can also create table styles? They're really handy for ensuring that all your tables look the same, eg same lining, shading and font.

It's a good idea to create a table layout exactly as you want it, then save it as your default table style. That way, every time you insert a new table it will already have the table attributes you want.

Here are some more table tools in Word that are particularly useful:

- ✓ For tables that run over more than one page, you can make heading rows appear at the top of every page, by ticking (in the table's properties) **Repeat as header row**.
- ✓ You can get a table's columns to automatically stretch and shrink to the optimum width for the contents, using **Autofit**.

- ✓ You can sort the contents of a table alphabetically, numerically, or by date, using **Table > Sort** (and it works for text outside tables as well).
- ✓ You can automatically convert body text to table text, and vice versa, using Word's **Convert Table to Text** and **Convert Text to Table** functions.

Minimise lining and shading

Minimise lines (such as table borders) and shading, and keep them as thin/light as possible. Especially with tables, lots of thick lines and dark shading create an ugly, pasty look and reduce legibility by drawing attention away from the words they contain.

Also bear in mind that people read across table columns, so avoid using vertical lining to separate columns lining if possible as it creates a series of visual hurdles for readers' eyes to jump across.

If you want a bit more visual separation between rows, your best choices are either light lines or alternate shading (what a graphic designer I once worked with memorably referred to as 'peppermint stripes'):

ISP	*Av speed*	*Cost*
A	54 Mbps	£28 million
B	36 Mbps	£17 million
C	24 Mbps	£12 million

ISP	*Av speed*	*Cost*
A	54 Mbps	£28 million
B	36 Mbps	£17 million
C	24 Mbps	£12 million

Table 1.1 Table styles

Keeping tables looking light and consistent is where table styles come in very handy.

As well as tables, watch out for excessive lining in other layout elements. Too many horizontal lines (eg underlining as part of a heading style) can harm legibility by slicing your pages into horizontal chunks, which reduces vertical flow as people are reading down a page. On a website, where information can appear below the fold (ie where you have to scroll to see it), horizontal lines can even fool people into thinking they've reached the end of the page.

Use regular line spacing

If you're using Microsoft Word it's wise to make the line spacing for the Normal paragraph style the same above and below (eg 6 pt above, 6 pt below) to ensure an even amount of space above and below tables, graphics, and other document elements.

Also, make sure you demarcate paragraphs in one of the two following ways:

- Spacing above/below and no indents: This approach is called block form and is by far the commonest way of paragraphing in business writing and probably the most legible, and so your best choice.
- Each paragraph starting with an indent (except the first) and no spacing above/below: This style of paragraphing is rare in business writing. You're most likely to see it in magazines, newspapers and novels.

Never write paragraphs without either spacing or indents. It makes it hard (sometimes impossible) to tell where one paragraph ends and the next starts. It's also considered a typographical error and makes your writing look unprofessional.

For headings, it's a good idea to use the Normal spacing or a multiple thereof (eg 12 pt above, 6 pt below). Ideally, give headings more space above than below so they remain visually anchored to the paragraph they apply to.

Consider too not only the spacing above/below paragraphs but also between lines: what's known as leading (pronounced *ledding*), so called because in the days of hot-metal printing the extra line spacing was created with thin strips of lead. Leading lets in a bit of visual fresh air: without it, text tends to look cramped. A typical amount of leading is 1.15 times the font size but what looks good also depends on the typeface.

Also bear in mind that the more leading you have, the greater the gap you're likely to need between paragraphs to provide a noticeable contrast with spacing within paragraphs.

Consider line length

Opinions differ on the ideal line length (or 'measure', as it's called if determined by characters per line), but an oft-quoted guideline is that for print the measure should be between 40 and 70 characters (roughly eight to twelve words), and slightly shorter for online text.

The problem with measures over 70 characters is that text becomes fatiguing to read, because our eyes have a long way to jump when we finish one line and move to the next – and there's a risk we'll skip up or down a line by mistake. And measures under 40 characters are hard to read as well, because phrases are chopped up between lines.

To get an optimal line length, you have several variables to play with: font, margins, and columns/tables (but one column only is usually best). And if your lines tend to be long, you can reduce the line-skip risk by increasing leading. If you're using Microsoft Word, you can get an auto-count of the number of characters in a line by selecting a line then using **Tools > Word Count**.

Minimise columns

As we've just seen, text in short lines can be hard to understand – a good reason for avoid multi-column layouts. Another reason is that text can easily get misaligned across columns. So unless you're producing a document where columns are vital, avoid them.

Avoid fancy text wrapping

If you're using Microsoft Word, avoid using any text-wrapping setting other than the default of **Wrap Text > In Line With Text**.

In Word, text wrapping around objects is very slippery in that if you add or delete text, the object and text tend to slide all over the place. An expert Word user can probably sort out the mess, but average Word users probably can't. Best play safe.

Use boilerplate text

If you regularly produce documents that are variations on a theme, such as policies, consider creating a template with standardised headings and body text – and guidelines on what information writers should provide.

It's best to make any boilerplate text as generic as you can get away with, to reduce or even eliminate the need for manual adjustments (and to shorten the text):

✗ Our recommendations for *[client name]* are …
✓ We recommend …
✗ Actuaries [*specialising / specializing*] in health insurance *[potential UK/ US conflict]*
✓ Health-insurance actuaries

Avoid creating pointless templates

Avoid creating more templates than necessary. For example, you don't need a different template for each phase of a project: business case template, high-level requirements template, project initiation template, and so on. Rather than forcing readers into a 'hermit crab' approach of constantly moving text into ever-bigger shells as a project progresses (which is time-consuming and error-prone), just create fewer but bigger shells.

Another classic example of needless templates is 'getting started' user guides that provide nothing more than a subset of the main manual – a far smarter approach is to have all the material in the same document, but with the 'getting started' material as the introductory chapter.

Make templates findable

To ensure that readers can always find your template (or even know that it exists) it's wise to include the template's URL in documents created from the template.

PICK A FILENAME

Your document is only one out of many, possibly hundreds or even thousands, and it's essential that not just you can find it but also everyone else. And filenames are critical to how findable your document is. The following sections give tips on how to choose a good filename.

Make filenames obvious but not redundant

The best filenames make the document's contents obvious from the filename alone. That said, avoid anything redundant, eg XYZ_status-report_*document*.docx.

Adopt a consistent taxonomy

A filename's not just useful for identifying documents but also showing how each document relates to others. It's therefore wise to adopt a taxonomy (naming and classification scheme), preferably using standard elements arranged from generic to specific. For example:

Syntax: <Client>_<topic>_<doc type>_<date>
Example: MegaCorp_annual_report_2020

To appreciate the power of a consistent taxonomy, think of how categorising millions of species of plants and animals relies on a mere seven elements:

Syntax: <Kingdom> <phylum> <class> <order> <family> <genus> <species>
Example: Animalia > Chordata > Mammalia > Primates > Lemuridae > Lemur > catta (ring-tailed lemur)

Never version by filename

Avoid putting in filenames any information likely to change, such as version numbers (Document_v0.1, Document_v0.2, etc). For example, if you have a filename such as XYZ_status-report_draft and later change it to XYZ_status-report_final, any links to that filename will break. Also, you risk causing havoc not only for yourself but also for others, if other people have used the link in their emails and documents without your knowing.

It's far better to manage the volatile information (version number, status, etc) using some other method such as SharePoint properties.

If you must use dates, use yyyy-mm-dd

As just mentioned, it's wise to avoid putting volatile information in filenames, eg the date a draft was written. The only sensible reason for dates in filenames is when the date refers to the content rather than the document per se, such as a report for a meeting held on a specific date.

If you must put a date in a filename, it's best to use the yyyy-mm-dd format, because:

✓ Documents appear in lists chronologically:

  Company-X_minutes_2019-12-13
  Company-X_minutes_2019-12-06
  Company-X_minutes_2019-11-27

✓ You avoid ambiguity between different date formats, eg UK (dd-mm-yyyy) v US (mm-dd-yyyy)

Avoid spaces with SharePoint

If you use SharePoint as your document repository, avoid spaces in filenames. The reason is that URLs can't contain spaces so SharePoint replaces any spaces in a document's filename with %20 – and this makes the URL ugly and hard to read.

The commonest ways to avoid spaces in filenames are to replace them with underscores (my_filename) or hyphens (my-filename), or to run words together and use initial caps to distinguish each word (MyFilename).

And avoid using special characters in filenames, as SharePoint can't handle them: letters, numbers, underscores and hyphens are about your lot.

DESIGN THE STRUCTURE

Before writing a single paragraph, you need to design your document's structure.

Create a wireframe of headings

The best way to write a document is top-down, building a skeleton of headings on which you can build the muscle and flesh of your body text. A sign of a well-designed document is that it has a strong narrative spine: readers can grasp the entire narrative of the document from its headings alone.

Why start with just an outline? The same reasons that a web designer creates a wireframe first or a moviemaker creates a storyboard before shooting scenes: you can shape and shuffle the main elements until everything's covered and in the right order, without getting bogged down in the details; and you're less likely to forget anything or to drift off course. Outlines are also incredibly useful if the document's going to be written by several people, because you can parcel out the work per section.

Even if you're updating an existing document, you'll probably find it easiest to create the outline first: especially if the existing document's messy. Picking your way through someone else's jumbled content is like trying to move furniture into an already cluttered room. In contrast, moving your material into an empty outline is as practical as putting your 'cutlery and crockery' cartons in the kitchen, 'books and DVDs' cartons in the living room, and 'clothes and bedsheets' cartons in the bedroom – everything's in the right place before you start unpacking it.

Here's how you do it. First, determine your top-level themes, how best to 'slice' your information: that gives you your chapters (Heading 1s). Then determine how best to 'dice' each chapter into sections of their own: that's your Heading 2s. For a big document, you might need to go down to Heading 3. But resist any temptation to go deeper or you risk getting lost in the details, which defeats the whole point of working top-down. (Once you start drafting you might choose to go deeper than Heading 3, but even then there are ways to avoid doing so, such as tucking low-level sections into tables: more on this later.)

If mind maps, flowcharts, decision trees or other visual/nonlinear approaches work better for you, go for it. But what you want to finish with is a cascade of headings with no body text.

Start with purpose and audience

The first thoughts readers have about an unfamiliar document are:

- 'What's it about?'
- 'Do I need to read it?'

So start your document with answers to both. Here, you'll feel the benefit of having completed the first two steps in my recommended process because you'll know the answers already.

The conventional way to supply these answers this is to make your first chapter 'About this document' and give it 'Purpose' and 'Scope' sections. It's a pragmatic solution but a bit dull, so for certain documents (particularly more informal ones) you might want to be less explicit. But the information does need to be there, even if it's only implied.

Find the story

To quote the story consultant Lisa Cron, human brains are 'wired for story' and storytelling is, '... nature's way of seducing us into paying attention'. We want to know what happens next, and *why*. Movies and commercial novels play on our addiction to story with what's called the three-act structure: setup, confrontation (or elaboration) and resolution. And you can do something similar in a business document: introduce, expand and conclude.

In fact, a good sign you've got the structure right is that the table of contents reads like a story. Readers often want to skip to a specific section, and it's your job to ensure they can find it from the table of contents. Let's look now at some ways you can organise your document to provide a strong narrative structure, along with examples:

- Generic to specific (eg a project implementation document that starts with an executive summary of the business case followed by the business plan, then chapters detailing the project phases)
- Readership (eg an underwriting guide with separate chapters for each type of person involved in underwriting: actuaries, underwriters, client support, etc)
- Familiar to unfamiliar (eg a report explaining a company's restructuring that starts with the current structure before detailing the changes)
- Simple to complex (eg a software guide that starts with a 'getting started' chapter before diving into the more advanced features)
- Alphabetical (eg reference material such as a parts list, or glossaries and indexes – for anything procedural, alphabetical sorting tends to produce an arbitrary structure and is best avoided)
- Chronological (eg instructions, or documents describing a project's phases)
- Ranking (eg a risk report, with risks listed by highest to lowest severity)

One feature common to pretty well all of the above structuring principles is that they help readers build on what they already know, ie they all support the spiral approach (aka progressive disclosure or given-new principle) we touched on earlier. A further advantage of given-new is that you can explain new topics using the formula 'B is the same as A, *except that*' and this benefits everyone:

✓ Your readers benefit, because their cognitive load is reduced
✓ You as the writer benefit, because you don't have to repeat material

Make headings unambiguous and unique

Make every heading unambiguous and unique, eg 'Overview of validating the pricing procedure' rather than just 'Overview'. Above all, avoid 'Introduction' sections in every chapter and go straight into the body text after a chapter heading. Why? Several reasons:

- It's obvious that the text coming straight after a chapter heading is the introduction to that chapter, meaning the 'Introduction' heading is redundant.
- You don't want a whole string of redundant 'Introduction' headings clogging up your table of contents.
- If you need to cross-refer to the start of a chapter, a cross-reference to the chapter heading itself is more meaningful than a cross-reference to a section called 'Introduction'.

Be aware that a heading can look informative when really it's not. Take 'Escalation procedure' – it's a procedure and it's about escalation! Isn't that enough? Well, no, because it doesn't say what it's an escalation procedure *for*. What you need is something such as 'Escalating security breaches'.

Or take a situation such as having a chapter called 'Risk calibrations' where you want a section on methodology. You might think there's no point wasting words spelling out 'Methodology for risk calibrations' rather than simply saying 'Methodology' but you'd be wrong and here's why:

- What if the 'Methodology' heading appears on a different page from the chapter heading? You lose the context.
- What if you use the heading as a cross-reference in another chapter? Suppose, for example, that a section called 'Methodology' from the 'Risk calibrations' chapter appears in the 'Validation' chapter: readers will assume (wrongly) that the section is about the methodology for validation rather than for calibration.

  A further advantage of context-rich headings is removing the need for section numbering, such as *2.1* Methodology and *3.1* Methodology.

  Incidentally, if you cross-refer using heading numbers, it's best to include the heading text as well. That way, it's easier for you (and readers) to see whether the cross-reference is actually pointing to the right section:

  ? The univariate approach is explained in section 5.1.4

  ✓ See 5.1.4 Univariate approach

- What if a reader goes straight to a section without reading what came before? Especially when browsing the web, people rarely read in a linear fashion from beginning to end – so for them (to quote technical author Mark Baker), 'Every page is page one'. And headings are vital for helping sections make sense on their own.

Make headings easy to scan

Break up any sequences of headings starting with the same word. For example, try scanning these headings:

Validation methods

    Validation options
    Validation decisions

Calibration methods

    Calibration options
    Calibration decisions

Now see how much easier you can scan the headings when they're rewritten as follows:

Validation methods

    Options for validation
    Decisions for validation

Calibration methods

    Options for calibration
    Decisions for calibration

As well as varying the initial words, the second version has the advantage of revealing that the two sections have the same pattern (Introduction > Options / Decisions).

'Ease of scanning' is also a reason for not starting any sentences in lists (be they bullets, table rows or whatever) with generic words such as *the* and *a*.

Use gerunds (-ing words) for processes and procedures

For any sections describing anything procedural, a good trick is to use a gerund (*-ing* word) in the heading, because gerunds immediately cue readers into the fact that what you're describing is a series of actions, eg *creating*, *designing* or *modifying*.

For example, suppose you saw a section headed 'Risk assessment' – without going to the section, you'd have no way of telling whether it describes the results of a risk assessment, plans for assessing risks, or the process itself. But if the heading were 'Assessing risks' you'd know immediately.

Some people indicate procedures using headings starting with 'How to' – but the problem (as we saw in the previous section) is that repeated words make headings hard to scan. Another approach that does work, however, is using imperatives (verbs forming commands), as in the headings I've used for the major steps in creating a document: *Consider* what outcomes you want, *Research* your readers, and so on.

A couple of caveats about gerunds: first, they can be ambiguous, eg 'Reporting requirements' could mean 'How to report requirements' or 'Requirements for reporting'. In such cases, it's best to rewrite the heading to avoid the ambiguity. Second, while gerund phrases work for headings they make terrible subjects for sentences, because they put a huge cognitive burden on your readers. Compare:

✗ Running down the corridor and crashing through the swing doors, the doctor slammed into an orderly pushing a patient on a gurney.

Feel how your brain aches having to hold in suspension all that information before you get to the sentence's subject (*doctor*). And feel how much easier you digest who's doing what in this rewrite:

✓ The doctor ran down the corridor, crashed through the swing doors, and slammed into an orderly pushing a patient on a gurney.

Balance section length and complexity

If a chapter feels huge and has an unwieldy number of sections and subsections, consider promoting the major sections to chapters in their own right. Similarly, consider absorbing excessively small chapters into a bigger chapter.

If you're doing this in Microsoft Word, you'll find it helpful to use **View > Outline**, whereby you can collapse and telescope a document by heading level, reorder sections by dragging and dropping their headings into new positions, and promote/demote sections (eg promote a Heading 3 section to Heading 2 level).

Append supplementary information

If information is of only secondary interest to most readers, such as sample reports or background research, consider putting it in an appendix. As with the rest of your document, appendices need to be well organised, eg alphabetically or following the order in which the topics appear in the main text.

WRITE THE FIRST DRAFT

When writing your first draft, it's a good idea to stick with the top-down approach you used to wireframe your document's structure. The first reason for doing so is that you can sort out your main ideas without getting lost in the details. To use a great word coined by Michael Ondaatje in his novel *The English Patient*, you're giving yourself space for 'thinkering' – exploring and discovering through a combination of thinking and tinkering. It's easier to get inventive when you allow yourself to play.

Second, it helps psychologically, especially with big documents. Instead of grappling with a huge monster, you're dealing with one manageable chunk at a time. I think of it as 'eating the aeroplane', in honour of the eccentric French entertainer Michel Lotito who 'ate' a series of implausible objects, including a Cessna 150 light aircraft (it took him two years, but he did it – in small chunks).

Third, you're much more likely to produce a dynamic flow of ideas clearly signposted by headings, paragraph breaks and other typographical landmarks such as tables. The preparation you did when researching your readers will have worked into your unconscious by now, and sprinting through the first draft helps you to maintain the momentum of your ideas.

For now, focus on getting the content properly structured and complete. In later stages you'll have plenty of opportunities to clarify your meaning, refine your style, fix your formatting, and do your final checks.

Put yourself in the right mindset

If you're bored or otherwise resenting writing a document, your negativity will taint the text and readers will sense it. Before you start writing, it's important to be feeling enthusiastic and genuinely wanting to help your readers.

Even if you find your working environment demotivating, you can always find satisfaction from writing because it's a great way to clarify your thinking, explore ideas, express yourself – and once you're enjoying writing, everyone benefits. Including you.

Think long, write fast, edit slowly

When tackling your first draft, it's wise to mull over what you want to say before you write a word. Why? Because you reduce the risk of false starts and hesitancies, that horrible feeling of writing and writing but getting nowhere. Read through your notes, pick out the things you need to cover, then let your mind roam over ways to tie your ideas together. Then blast through your first draft as fast as you can, trusting your unconscious to steer you in the right direction. (A good trick is to use your writing tool's zoom function to provide a psychological shift of emphasis: zoom out when burning through your fast draft; then zoom in later, when you want a cool-headed look at the details when editing.)

If writing fast feels scary and the blank page is intimidating you, just get your words down anyway; they're not carved in stone and you can (and will) progressively improve them in later drafts. The dirty little secret of 'effortless' prose is that it's almost invariably the result of re-rewriting.

If you get stuck or you're unhappy with what you've written, that's fine. Just park it for the next draft, perhaps adding a 'note to self' (eg 'Ask Fred', 'Needs expanding', 'Check dates', 'Swap order?') before moving on. Why park it rather than thrash it out there and then?

First, it's hard to be inspired when your inner critic is nagging you to get your words perfect. For early drafts it's best to give free rein to your right-brain creativity: and the editing stages will give your left-brain critic plenty of opportunities to take over.

Second, when you pass by the problem in the next draft, you'll usually understand it better: you have the big picture and the benefit of hindsight, and your unconscious will have had time to work on it. Writing is often about understanding your subject matter on the way out rather than on the way in. For this reason, introductions are ironically easiest to write if you do them last.

Follow every heading with body text

Always provide some body text between headings, to provide context. For example, don't jump straight from a chapter heading to a section heading without explaining what the chapter's about.

To appreciate the importance of context, think of how most movies start: with a panning shot sweeping the scene ('Ah, so we're in rainy London'), a tracking shot ('Ah, out of that crowd the person I need to watch is the one hurrying into an office under an umbrella'), then a zoom into a person's face ('Ah, that's probably the person whose story we're going to be told.') Your introduction after the heading is like the panning and tracking shots to set the scene and orient your readers.

Here's another example of the power of context – what connects the following and what's each one stand for?

- libra
- romance
- yam

Confused? Now suppose I introduced the list by writing, 'The following are all anagrams of British prime ministers' – I bet you'd find each one fairly fast; and even faster if I gave you even more context, such as that they're all prime ministers who've served in the twenty-first century, arranged in chronological order (Blair, Cameron, May). But without a frame of reference (or schema, as cognitive psychologists call them) you're utterly lost.

If you're interested in reading more about schemas, check out this short article from OpenLearn, the Open University's free learning pages: https://tinyurl.com/OpenLearnSchemas

Use your headings as your roadmap

Thinking of headings as signposts helps you create a clear narrative path. The heading above your current chunk of body text provides your starting point, and the heading beneath it your next destination.

Grab your readers early

If you don't want your readers to skip sections, you've got to grab their attention as early as possible. Numerous eye-tracking tests have validated that most people skim-read in what's called an F-pattern: across the top (the top bar of the F), a little bit less further down (the lower bar of the F) then tailing off.

Pole position, then, is the very first word, followed by the rest of the heading or first sentence. Another critical 'top bar of the F' is the subject line of emails. Think how swiftly you skip, junk or delete emails with meaning-starved subject lines such as 'Tomorrow's meeting' or 'Feedback'. If you don't want your own emails to suffer the same fate, give them an impactful subject line. It's especially important when you need the recipient to do something (eg 'Lloyd's submission – need response by 4pm').

Also, front-load your body text with the most important stuff – remember that people often read emails only in the preview pane or on their mobiles, and might delete your email without even seeing the most important bit.

Ways to grab your readers' attention early include:

✓ Stating a problem that's meaningful to them, with a hint or promise that you'll explain the solution as well (this technique is so important it has its own section later on)
✓ Saying something to their advantage (such as 'Slash your gas bill by 15%') or something that worries them ('Is your gas supplier ripping you off?')
✓ Supplying a startling or impressive fact
✓ Giving an apt quotation

✓ Telling a personal anecdote
✓ Sharing human-interest news

The last of these is usually the most attention grabbing of all. Think of gossip, of chats around the office water cooler. In fact, applying a water-cooler test – or what's more commonly called the 'so what?' test – is useful when deciding what's worth writing in newsletters, case studies, press releases and other marketing material. For example, can you imagine someone rushing to the water cooler to whisper in a colleague's ear: 'Megasoft have just released the latest version of their best-in-class, disruptive financial-markets data platform!'? Nor can I.

Keep working top-down

Remember the organising principles from the outlining stage? Well, these work not just for headings but also for paragraphs and even sentences. Take the principle of organising by main point to specifics – if you look at any newspaper or magazine article you'll see this principle in action. It's what journalists call the inverted pyramid (or triangle) and it looks like this:

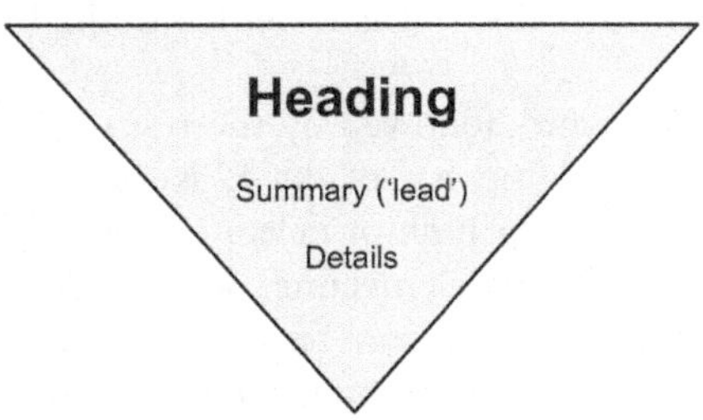

Figure 1.2 Inverted pyramid (or triangle)

Let's use a made-up tabloid story as an example and I'm sure the format will be immediately familiar to you:

Love rat dumps X Factor star

Emma Bimbella in tears after cage-fighter Nick Scrote dumps her on Twitter

Last night, Emma was devastated when she came off stage after the X Factor semi-finals to learn that her cage-fighter fella's 20,000 Twitter followers knew she'd been dumped before she did. Talking about her heartbreak, Emma told reporters that...

Figure 1.3 Headline, lead and story

If you have a meaningful heading followed by a succinct sentence or two that captures the topic's essence, what journalists call the 'lead' (as in something that leads the story), all readers will find your ideas easier to grasp, and skim-readers will appreciate not having to wade through details to find your point. You'll know from your own news-reading habits that you read till your interest flags then you bail out; pyramiding means your readers can do the same.

And remember the F-pattern for how readers skim text? Pyramiding is a great tool for shaping your text such that readers not only grasp your main points but also linger long enough to read more than the headline.

Another organisational principle that works just as well in your body text as it does in your headings is 'familiar to unfamiliar'. As you'll remember from our earlier discussions of the spiral approach (aka progressive disclosure or given-new principle), readers find it easier to grasp something new if they already understand the context:

✓ Validating results for this quarter is the same as for last quarter *except that …*

Also remember that the 'same as … except that' formula helps you as well as your readers, because you avoid having to regurgitate old material – meaning less to write, less to maintain, and less risk of the same thing getting said in different ways in different places.

What about organising by chronology? This is especially handy when giving instructions. Imagine, for example, you're learning to drive and you read a handbook that says:

> The steering wheel controls the direction of the car. The gear stick is operated in conjunction with the clutch, which is the left pedal. The ignition is where you put the key to start the engine. The accelerator is the pedal on the right. The handbrake is the stick to your left.

Would that description enable you to drive? I doubt it. OK, suppose the handbook said this instead:

1 Put the key in the ignition.
2 Turn the key.
3 Press the clutch (left pedal) and move the gear stick to first gear (top left).
4 Release the handbrake.
5 Press the accelerator (right pedal).

Why's the second example so much easier to follow? Several reasons:

- ✓ The numbers show you the order in which to do things.
- ✓ Each step starts with a verb (ie an action) rather than a noun (ie a description).
- ✓ When people are switching between reading and doing the steps, the numbers help them find the next step.

A good trick is to perform the process/procedure yourself and write it up as you go. You can then go one step better by asking a colleague to follow your instructions and say out loud anything they don't understand. Doing so means that:

- ✓ You can be sure you haven't missed any vital steps and that your instructions work.
- ✓ You describe the steps in a natural, task-oriented way.
- ✓ You're simultaneously checking that the process or procedure works as expected.

The main thing to remember about instructions is to keep them simple, natural and active – how you'd explain a task to someone who asked you in person. If you want a model to follow, look at a cookery book:

- ✗ An omelette is produced by whisking and heating eggs
- ✓ To make an omelette, crack eggs, whisk, add oil to pan …

Finally, here's an organisational principle we didn't discuss for headings but which is incredibly powerful in the body of your document: needs, benefits, features. It's a classic technique used by copywriters, and it works like this: first you describe a *need*, then explain the *benefits* of a solution to that need, and only then do you describe the solution's *features*. Or, to put it more bluntly, no one cares about features until you've convinced them that they've a problem to solve, *then* that the features you're trying to sell them would solve their problem best.

To take a simple example, suppose you work in a hardware store and a customer's walking past the electric drills. Here's a smart way to get a sale:

YOU: 'Hello, and what brought you to the store today?'
CUSTOMER: 'Well, I've got these bookshelves I need to put up.'
YOU: 'Books are surprisingly heavy – even small paperbacks weigh about 15kg per linear metre. So for safety you must secure your shelving to the walls. Ready-assembled shelving or flat-pack? Partition wall or load-bearing?'

CUSTOMER: 'Just planks of wood. I'm making them myself. And it's a load-bearing wall.'

YOU: 'So you'll need some decent masonry bits.'

CUSTOMER: 'I've already got a drill.'

YOU: 'Does your drill have a screwdriver attachment? That's really handy for screwing your planks together. And how heavy is the drill?'

CUSTOMER: 'Dunno, it's quite old. It's my dad's.'

YOU: 'Older models tend to be heavy and your arms will tire holding a heavy drill for any length of time, risking an accident. And your arms will really ache if you've got to tighten all those screws by hand. So if you *do* decide to treat yourself to your own drill, I'd go for one that's lightweight. Cordless as well, so you don't have to worry about how far away your power socket is. Like this one. It's less than 5kg and cordless. Also, it's got a range of torque settings, which means it can handle the heavy masonry work but also put your screws in without stripping their heads. Plus it's 20% off for this week only.'

CUSTOMER: 'Actually, my dad's drill isn't great …'

Needs, benefits, features: in that order and with everything from the *customer's* viewpoint. Notice too how the salesperson *shows* their expertise through their knowledgeable questions, rather than *telling* the customer they're an expert.

Now compare the smart approach with a counterproductive one:

SALESPERSON: 'Hey, you must be after an electric drill! I'm an expert on drills and I can tell you this model's really cool. It's on special offer, it weighs less than 5kg, it's cordless—'

CUSTOMER: 'Er, I was just walking through to the white goods section. I'm actually looking for a washing machine.' (To friend and out of earshot of the salesperson) 'I do actually want to buy a drill, but I can't stand being hassled by cocky salespeople.'

In other words, pushing features rather than addressing needs not only fails to convert reluctant buyers but can also turn off potential buyers. It's the number one reason (along with boasting, which we'll examine in detail later) that bad sales copy fails:

✗ Megasoft's feature-rich software leads the market in …

✓ Finding it hard to keep track of your clients' details? Need to collate data across multiple platforms? Imagine the time and errors you'd save by aggregating all your client data with one click in an easy-to-use, web-based form. Megasoft's GoldProspect …

In summary, lead with the need, and prove your credentials by framing your message in such a way that you show you understand the person's problems and how best to fix them.

'Needs, benefits, features' is great not just for selling but also for explaining. Why? Because it saves you from getting bogged down in details and forgetting to give the context – which leaves readers wondering, 'Why are you telling me this?'

Think back to our cookery book analogy: not 'When making a meringue, take your eggs out of the fridge about two hours before you start' (*why?*) but 'The secret of a good meringue [need] is warm eggs because they whisk better than refrigerated eggs [benefit], so take them out of the fridge about two hours before you start [solution].'

If you're struggling to flip features to benefits, use the magic phrase 'which means that':

- You have a dedicated project manager, *which means that* you will have a single point of contact and regular updates.
- The new hardware is 20% faster, *which means that* you can generate the same number of simulations faster than before, or more simulations in your current timeframe.

The need-benefit approach operates even at the sentence level:

✗ See Appendix A (page 37) *[why?]* for the year-end results.
✓ For the year-end results, see Appendix A (page 37).

A similar copywriting trick is AIDA (attention, interest, desire, action):

1 Grab their attention
2 Make them interested
3 Create desire
4 Make them act

Smooth the ride between sentences

By working top-down, you should have a clear sense of direction between the various topics and main points you want to cover. Your job now is to carry your readers as smoothly as possible from one sentence to the next.

One extremely effective way to carry your readers smoothly from sentence to sentence is to apply what's called referential continuity, a referent being the thing that a word refers to: for example, in the phrase *this book*, 'book' is the referent of 'this'.

But what exactly is referential continuity? To understand what it is, first imagine a row of dominoes arranged haphazardly, something such as this:

5|4 2|6 1|5 3|2 4|1

Try remembering the sequence, and see how hard it is compared to remembering dominoes arranged in order:

1|2 2|3 3|4 4|5 5|6

Referential continuity is essentially this 'arranging your dominoes' principle applied to words in sentences, and it makes your text far easier to understand. Compare:

✗ An insurance policy is a contract between an insurer and *insured*. The *policyholder* (as the insured is called) is insured for *losses*. *Premiums* are paid to cover these losses.
✓ An insurance policy is a contract between an insurer and *insured*. The *insured* is called the policyholder, who pays *premiums*. These *premiums* cover the policyholder for losses.

A further advantage of 'getting your dominoes in order' is that whereas out-of-order paragraphs force you to repeat the subjects and objects of sentences, ordered paragraphs don't – meaning you can tighten your text by cutting the repetitions:

✗ An insurance policy is a contract between an insurer and <u>insured. The insured</u> is called the policyholder, who pays <u>premiums. These premiums</u> cover the policyholder for losses.
✓ An insurance policy is a contract between an insurer and *insured* (aka policyholder), who pays *premiums* to cover losses.

Also, as Yellowlees Douglas points out in *The Reader's Brain: How Neuroscience Can Make You a Better Writer*, the power of referential continuity shows why the hoary old adage to vary your word choice is such a terrible idea. Use two or more words to describe the same thing and you not only knock your dominoes for six but can also fool your readers into thinking you're talking about something new instead of what they know already.

A second way to carry readers smoothly from sentence to sentence is using 'transitions' – words, phrases or sentences that signpost the path of your argument. For example:

- Amplification (especially, even more)
- Cause (because, therefore)
- Comparison (similarly, likewise)
- Conclusion (finally, in summary)
- Contrast (but, yet, however)

- Example (for instance)
- Location (ahead, behind, above)
- Result (hence, so)
- Sequence (first … second, initially, finally)
- Time (now, meanwhile, before, later)

A few caveats: the better you landscape your prose, the fewer signposts your readers will need. Never use fake signposts such as a *therefore* where there's no causality. And go easy on words such as *furthermore*, *nevertheless* and *thus*, which risk making your prose read like a bad undergrad essay.

Transitions work within sentences as well as between them. As Joseph M Williams and Joseph Bizup observe in *Style: Lessons in Clarity and Grace*, many complicated sentences can be simplified into one of the following patterns:

- X because Y
- If X, then Y
- Although X, Y

For example:

✗ The financial loss is the result of weak risk controls
✓ We lost money *because* our risk controls were weak

Of all transitions, *because* is probably the most powerful. Returning again to Yellowlees Douglas and her insightful book *The Reader's Brain: How Neuroscience Can Make You a Better Writer*, '… we read faster and recall content better when sentences use transitions that explicitly flag causation'. As she also points out, we even infer causality when it's not stated. For example, suppose you read:

> It started raining. Tom ran down the stairs.

Most people will assume that the rain *causes* Tom to run down the stairs. But Tom's reasons might be entirely different. He might not even be in the same place or time as the rain. Imagine, for example, if these two sentences came from a novel and 'Tom ran down the stairs' belonged in a new chapter or paragraph:

> It started raining.
> Tom ran down the stairs.

This brings us neatly to the matter of moving smoothly not between sentences but between paragraphs, where the transition needs to be stronger. One of the most effective approaches is asking a question in one paragraph that you answer in the next one. Another is starting a new paragraph with a recap of the previous one. As Sam Leith observes, in *Write to the Point*, stand-up comics use this recap technique to great effect by weaving in references to earlier jokes. 'Callbacks' (as they're known) build rapport and, when handled well, build increasingly big laughs as well. Novelists too use the recap technique, and the beauty is that if you describe something well the first time round you need give your readers only the gentlest of nudges for everything you told them earlier to come flooding back.

An extreme form of recapping, often used by journalists, is closing an article with something you said at the very beginning. I did this myself in an article on looping, which is a technique whereby a musician plays something live, records it in real time, then loops it to produce a riff to improvise over. My article started with …

> Auditory repetition is in our blood. Literally. The first sounds we ever heard were our mother's heartbeat, her breathing and intestinal sounds. A typical foetus responds to sound stimulation at around twenty-six weeks.

… and ended with

> Auditory repetition is in our blood. Literally. The first sounds…

… thereby showing in words the very looping the article was about. It's rare you'll get an opportunity to finish piece of writing as self-referentially as this, but when you can 'loop the loop' (as Sam Leith calls it) it provides a very gratifying finish for writer and reader alike.

Use paragraphing to group ideas

We've seen how to move smoothly between paragraphs, but how do you decide where the paragraph breaks should come in the first place?

The best rule of thumb is to think of paragraphs as chunking ideas into logical units. And, as the earlier 'It started raining / Tom ran down the stairs' example shows, having sentences in the same paragraph that *don't* belong together can lead readers to infer causality where none exists.

Here's an example of good v bad paragraphing. The words in each column are identical, the only difference being where the paragraphs break, and your job is simply to decide which feels easiest to grasp:

We assumed that sales in the first quarter would match the fourth quarter of last year. But we underestimated pre-Christmas demand. Also, January sales slashed margins. This means we need to increase sales for this quarter by 20%.	We assumed that sales in the first quarter would match the fourth quarter of last year. But we underestimated pre-Christmas demand. Also, January sales slashed margins. This means we need to increase sales for this quarter by 20%.

The difference is subtle, but you probably found the version on the right easier to grasp. Why? Look at how the paragraphing groups the information:

Background + part of the problem Rest of the problem + recommendation	Background Problem Recommendation

In other words, keep together sentences that elaborate on the same idea, then create a new paragraph when you move to the next idea. To use an analogy from TV, the example on the left is a bit like those annoying advert breaks that interrupt a scene mid-action, whereas the one on the right is like a proper scene shift. In short: complete a scene/paragraph before you move to the next.

Other factors to consider when deciding where to put your paragraph breaks are context and layout: context, in that emails (for example) require shorter paragraphs than long documents, because of people's tendency to skim-read emails; and layout, in that a short-looking paragraph will become much longer when squashed into a table or newspaper-style column.

Paragraphing is also great for emphasising ideas silently. For example, compare these two versions of the same message:

All departments must produce a status report. *Note that 31 December is the deadline.*	All departments must produce a status report. The deadline is 31 December.

See how the warning on the right stands out more, despite using fewer words and no italics?

That was two versions of the same message. Now let's look at three, to understand another way in which paragraphing can be useful for emphasising information:

All departments must produce a status report. *Note that 31 December is the deadline.*	All departments must produce a status report. The deadline is 31 December.	All departments must produce a status report by 31 December.

You're much more likely to remember the date in versions 2 and 3 than version 1. The reason is that the end word in a sentence is the one best remembered (*recency effect*), the start word second-best (*primacy effect*) and what's in the middle is what's most likely to be forgotten – a set of effects collectively known as the *serial-position effect.*

Look how much weaker Churchill's famous wartime quote would have been with 'never' in the middle of the sentence instead of at the start:

✗ In the field of human conflict, *never* was so much owed by so many to so few

✓ *Never* in the field of human conflict was so much owed by so many to so few

Group and sort ideas with tables

Ideas often relate to each other vertically (one idea followed by another) and horizontally (elaborations of each idea) – and tables are often better at showing this relationship than body text or bulleted lists. Any text comparing things (eg pros v cons) is usually best as a table, and any words or phrases you find yourself repeating in body text often provide a clue to table headings.

Tabulating is also great for helping you to spot missing information. Suppose, for example, you're documenting a procedure involving different people or teams so you decide to present it in a table with 'Who' and 'Steps' columns. If one of the steps is missing the 'who', you'll spot the gap immediately when there's nothing to plug into the cell.

As an example of how to tabulate, let's take the following text:

> The benefits of product A are that it is fast and reliable. Its drawback is that it is expensive. Product B's benefit is that it is much cheaper than A, but it is slow and unreliable.

At first glance it's a straight comparison between products, but depending on how you tabulate the information you can choose which aspects of each product you're comparing. For example, you could focus on features:

Product	*Speed*	*Reliability*	*Cost*
A	✓	✓	✗
B	✗	✗	✓

Table 1.2 Tabulating by features

Or you could shift the focus to pros and cons:

Product	*Pros and cons*
A	✓ Fast ✓ Reliable ✗ Expensive
B	✓ Cheap ✗ Slow ✗ Unreliable

Table 1.3 Tabulating by pros v cons

As well as considering what you want to emphasise (which determines your columns, as we've seen above), consider how many columns and rows your choices will produce. For example, if you're creating a table on a portrait page and one choice gives twelve columns and five rows and the other five columns and twelve rows, the second option is the obvious choice.

Tables are also useful for compressing low-level subsections of body text into something easier to read. Anything at Heading 4 level or lower is usually best tidied up into a table, as any reader will struggle to keep track of the relationships between multiple sub-sub-subsections. Another option (particularly if the chapter containing the Heading 4s feels unwieldy) is to promote the Heading 2 section to chapter (ie Heading 1) level, then promoting all its sections up a level (ie Heading 3s become Heading 2s, and Heading 4s become Heading 3s).

A final point about tables: don't centre-justify any text, even column headings. The reason is that doing so creates irregular margins on both sides of the text, making the text harder to read and sometimes creating distracting shapes. Always left-align text, but if you have rows of numbers then right-align them as doing so makes numbers easier to read, helps to differentiate them from text, and is standard typographic practice.

Use bulleted lists wisely and sparingly

Bulleted lists are both friend and foe – friend in that they break up chunks of text, and foe in that they're often misused as a way of dumping unstructured content.

First, keep any bulleted lists short – more than five bullets and you're playing 'memory roulette' with a fully loaded gun. Why? Well, Miller's law (1956) states that our working memories can retain only 'the magical number seven, plus or minus two' – but more recent research (Cowan, 2010) suggests it's only three to five items. If you do have a long list of bullets and you absolutely have to include them all, one solution is to break the bullets into secondary lists. For example, suppose you're itemising all the types of fraud that a bank needs to consider and it runs to ten types: if some types relate to internal fraud and others to external fraud, you can categorise the fraud types as such to produce two shorter bulleted lists.

Second, provide a meaningful lead-in (aka 'stem') sentence. For example, rather than introducing a list of household items as 'Things' and expecting readers to work out what sorts of things you're listing, you help your readers by introducing the list with something such as 'Items commonly found in a kitchen include …'

Third, make bulleted items and lists grammatically consistent with the lead-in sentence and each other. For example, can you spot what's wrong with the following list?

✗ Your writing should be: clear; conversational; write from the reader's viewpoint.

Did you notice the jarring inconsistency of 'Your writing should be … write from the reader's viewpoint'? Now compare that jarring effect with the smooth read you achieve when all your listed items are grammatically consistent with the lead-in sentence:

✓ Your writing should be: clear; conversational; written from the reader's viewpoint.

Finally, make sure bullets are truly better than body text, because:

- Breaking text into a bulleted list
- Doesn't automatically make it
- Easier to understand

Keep graphics relevant and close by

Use graphics to reinforce or illuminate the ideas in your text: graphics added purely for prettiness distract readers, because interpreting visual information requires a mental switch from reading. You may also leave your readers puzzling over the graphic's significance or even drawing their own (wrong) inferences.

Another important aspect of making graphics help rather than hinder is ensuring you always place them immediately after (or alongside) the text they relate to: 'as shown in the following diagram' is far clearer than 'see figure 5 on page 27', which forces readers to flick forwards and backwards.

Finally, here are three tips if you're writing a document that needs screenshots. First, avoid using screenshots for illustrating something that doesn't need to be shown as such. For example, if you want to illustrate a screen button within a line of text, rather than inserting a screenshot of the button it's far easier to create a character style that makes the text look like a button (or go ultra-simple and minimalist, and just use bold text).

Second, avoid very wide screenshots, as you either have to flip the layout to landscape (annoying for readers), or you have to stick to portrait but shrink the graphic till it fits (which reduces legibility). The solution? Either crop the shot to show only those bits of the screenshot that are important; or (if the location of elements within the screenshot is important) accept the lack of legibility but highlight any areas of interest with callouts such as bubbles or arrows, or use blurring or shading to draw the eye to the relevant part.

Third, if you're using Microsoft Word and need to produce screenshots with stuff painted on top (callout text, bubbles, arrows, whatever), create them in Microsoft Paint rather than using Word's graphics tools – this way you get a solid graphic with everything 'locked in' rather than independent elements that slide all over the place whenever the main graphic changes size or position.

End on cliffhangers

Earlier, we looked at the importance of grabbing your readers early. To keep your readers turning the pages, grab their interest at the end of each section as well as its start. And the best way to do that is to tease readers by ending on a cliffhanger. Good cliffhangers include questions, promises, or anything else that generates a mystery or sense of incompleteness. For example:

> Those are the barriers to sales, but how can we overcome them? Let's find out.

As well as arousing curiosity, cliffhangers play to the Zeigarnik effect: the human tendency to remember what's unfinished or interrupted rather than what's complete.

How to untangle a poor structure

We've looked at several ways to create a good structure, but suppose you're editing someone else's document and its structure's all over the place: how do you fix it? And how do you spot it's a mess to start with?

For me, there are two red flags that a document's structure is poor. The first is excessive cross-references, forcing readers to jump backwards and forwards rather than read in a linear fashion. The second is a tacked-on, oh-and-another-thing feel to the information: paragraphs crammed with unrelated topics; something stated a few paragraphs ago cropping up again out of context; bulleted lists that are jumbles of unrelated items. This problem is especially prevalent in older documents edited many times by different authors. If an author is lazy, unsure of the subject matter, or pressed for time, rather than replacing or blending information they're inclined to append it. You end up with what I call a 'coral-reef document', a document built up of layers of dead and calcified text disguising the small fringe of content that's still alive.

Also look out for the following signs of a poor structure *across* documents: material cut-and-pasted from one document to another; different versions of the same information; and lots of cross-references between documents, such as, 'Follow the processes described in documents X, Y and Z.'

If you find yourself having to untangle a bad structure, here's an effective approach:

1. Note what each sentence is trying to say, perhaps using a number scheme to identify themes and ideas relating to those themes (eg A1 for a sentence related to 'theme A, first idea').
2. Delete/merge sentences saying the same or similar things (eg if you've found several sentences you've marked A1).
3. Group the remaining sentences by the themes you've identified.
4. Put each theme in its own paragraph or under its own heading.
5. Use the techniques we've explored so far to smooth the flow between each sentence and paragraph.

REVISE FOR MEANING

Ernest Hemingway got it right when he said that 'The first draft of anything is shit' because most of the effort in making writing great is revision.

In fact, what makes great writers great is often their urge to obsessively revise: Hemingway himself famously admitted in an interview with *The Paris Review* that he rewrote the final page of *A Farewell to Arms* a staggering 39 times; Tolstoy's wife showed astonishing love and fortitude in handwriting at least eight copies of *War and Peace* for her husband, rewriting some passages up to 26 times; and Proust was still revising *In Search of Lost Time* on his deathbed.

Why's revision so important? Because it's *re-vision*, seeing what you didn't see the first time: seeing what's unclear, what's awkward, what's lifeless; seeing where your understanding of the topic stumbled, or at least where you fumbled in explaining it; seeing where you left something out or took the wrong path. In fact, by the time you're done with revising you should be sick of your own words. Cherish that feeling, because being fed up when editing helps you overcome first-draft euphoria, that deluded feeling of 'What a damn fine piece of writing this is!' Trust me – most writing only becomes 'damn fine' several revisions later.

There's no set order for what to fix per draft, but a pragmatic approach is one of progressive refinement: clarify your meaning (the most important thing to fix), improve your phrasing, fix your formatting, then polish. As you gain experience and skill you'll find you can fix multiple things at once. But for now, let's get cracking with the most important (and hence first) stage of editing: clarifying your meaning.

Remove anything irrelevant

Prune all irrelevant details; they slow your readers and can also confuse and mislead them, as shown by a riddle that goes:

> You are a bus driver with 37 passengers. At the first stop, ten people get off and seven get on; at the next stop, eight people get on and four get off … *(etc)*. Who was the driver?

People become so focused on calculating the final number of passengers (wrongly assuming it will be the riddle's question) they forget you started with, '*You* are a bus driver …' Misdirection can even cause people not to see something that's right in front of their eyes, a phenomenon known as inattentional blindness. For some mindboggling examples, see www.theinvisiblegorilla.com/videos.html.

This misdirection phenomenon explains why many presentations fail, those snoozefests where the speaker says things such as: 'In the fourth quartile, the aviation sector came in at −09.5% when our target was +1.3%, whereas solar energy was projected to be −1.4% but was +2.3% and marine was +0.7% compared to the +0.5% projected …' As an audience member you get so bamboozled by the numbers (especially when they're being read off a slide) that you miss the trends and who's going to remember all those numbers anyway?

A smarter approach for presentations is to limit what you say to something as simple as, 'Aviation fell by nearly 10%, but solar energy and marine both rose slightly' and support what you're saying with a few intuitive graphics. You can always give people the numbers as a handout – *after* your presentation.

As well as taxing people's memories, overloading people with irrelevant details leads to anxiety and poor choices. As the psychologist Daniel Goleman explains in his book *Focus*, this happens because the dorsolateral prefrontal cortex (brain region associated with reasoning) gives up, giving free rein to the amygdala (fear centre of the brain). This fear is commonly referred to as 'analysis paralysis' or 'the paradox of choice' and it leads people to make either bad choices or no choice at all.

Similarly, if you're writing instructions, remember that readers usually want just enough information to get the job done. Imagine installing a new Blu-ray player and wondering, 'How do I get surround sound?' – you grab the instruction booklet but instead of 'Press this button' you get a sound engineer's thesis on every flavour of Dolby, or patronising sales patter such as, 'Congratulations on buying your Blu-ray! We are a leading supplier of ...'

Incidentally, the relevance principle applies to advertising and marketing as well. Sales messages are much more convincing if you stick to the best arguments and leave out the barrel-scrapers.

Specify the doer (usually)

Ah, passives, the curse of much corporate writing and the bane of an editor's life. But they're not all bad – far from it. The oft-given writing tip to make all passive sentences active is simplistic because the passive voice does have roles to play, as we'll see in a moment. But first, what do we mean by 'active v passive voice'?

A sentence is in the active voice if the subject is doing something ('The dog bit the girl') and passive if the subject's having something done to it ('The girl was bitten by the dog' or simply 'the girl was bitten').

Active is usually easier to understand because cause and effect are in the right order (dog bit girl, subject-verb-object) whereas passive forces you to read backwards to work out the order of events. Another reason that active is good is that it requires an actor (dog) whereas the passive doesn't (girl bitten, by creature unknown). Similarly:

✗ All validation results must be signed off *[by whom?]*

For things such as policies, it's especially important to specify a doer because an instruction is only meaningful if it's clear who has to do it. Sometimes it's obvious: 'Keep off the grass' applies to you, matey – yes, you, and everyone else thinking of stepping on my beautifully manicured lawn. But most of the time it's not: 'A report needs to be written.' Does it? Not by me, mate.

One way in which passives are useful is for shifting the emphasis from *who* to *what*, but even in these cases it's often helpful to specify the doer. To return to our earlier example:

✓ Active (emphasises *who*): The executive committee must sign off all validation results

✓ Passive (emphasises *what* – but this time we're going to add *who*): All validation results must be signed off, *by the executive committee*

If the person or thing performing the action is unknown, implicit or less important than the object, it's OK not to specify the doer. This is the main reason that scientific papers tend to be written in the passive, eg 'DNA samples were extracted'. Similarly:

✓ Testing finished on Thursday

✓ Joe Biden was elected US president

Try turning the above sentences into the active and you'll see why it's so dumb to say that all passives need to be made active:

✗ The testers finished testing on Thursday *[well, duh, who else?]*

✗ The US electorate elected Joe Biden as president *[again, who else?]*

If the doer is irrelevant, avoid passive constructions that imply a doer exists:

✗ It is proposed *[reader thinks: by whom?]* that interest rates be raised to stimulate the economy

✓ Raising interest rates will stimulate the economy

Passives are also useful for (as the cognitive psychologist and linguist Steven Pinker puts it) introducing topics in the order in which a reader can absorb them. In the following example, notice how changing the first verb from active to passive makes the sentence easier to understand by keeping the entire sentence's focus on the same subject:

✗ Water, wind and tillage *cause* soil erosion, and this erosion affects crop yields
✓ Soil erosion *is caused by* water, wind and tillage, and affects crop yields

That's an example of passive and active verbs being combined to keep the focus on the same subject, but on other occasions you may need all active or all passive:

✗ (unfocused – active/passive) The board must approve the strategy and it must be implemented by the executive committee
✓ (focus on *who* – all active) The board must approve the strategy and the executive committee must implement it
✓ (focus on *what* – all passive) The strategy must be approved by the board and implemented by the executive committee

Another focus shift where the passive comes in handy is if you want to flip the viewpoint from *me* (the writer) to *you* (the reader):

- We've processed your order
- Your order's been processed

But avoid needless passives, which look verbose and sound evasive:

✗ Mistakes were made with your order
✓ We got your order wrong
✗ It was decided by the CRO …
✓ The CRO decided …

Even active sentences can be evasive if they deliberately leave out a significant doer. Take this sentence from an email by the then CEO of United Airlines, Oscar Munoz, in response to the scandal when a paying passenger who'd refused to give up his seat on an overbooked flight was dragged off the plane by Chicago Aviation security officers and left bloody and dazed:

✗ Our employees followed established procedures for dealing with situations like this.

That's all very well, think readers, but what were those (obviously flawed) procedures? And who insisted that they be followed despite common sense and human decency yelling the opposite?

Address ends, not means

Make sure you're clear about the difference between ends and means. A lot of corporate documentation is riddled with statements that confuse the two, statements such as:

✗ *In order to meet the requirements of the risk-management framework process*, it is necessary that all cybersecurity risks be recorded, assessed and mitigated

No, no, no, no, no! 'Meeting the requirements of a framework' is never the reason for doing anything – it's only ever the means:

✓ *To make our company's data as secure as possible*, all cybersecurity risks must be recorded, assessed and mitigated

Another example:

✗ *A process must be in place* to ensure that all data security breaches are reported to the cybersecurity team

Merely having a process (the means) won't achieve anything. Only *doing* something will:

✓ *You must* report all data security breaches to the cybersecurity team

Still not convinced? Imagine it in a domestic environment:

✗ A process must be in place to ensure that our children are collected from school when one of us is working late
✓ I'm working late, so remember to collect the kids from school

Plug hidden assumptions

Once we become experts at something, we lose our innocence as to how hard we found it ourselves when we first tried it. Take how to tie your shoelaces: if you think it's 'obvious', try writing instructions on how to do it. This loss of innocence, this inability to put ourselves in others' shoes, is commonly called 'the curse of knowledge' and it can wreak havoc by causing us to overlook information our readers need. Take an innocuous sentence such as this one:

Ann walked to the bank

What meaning did you attribute to the word 'bank'? Did you even consider that there might be more than one meaning? OK, now compare these two sentences:

- Ann walked to the bank, and took out £20 from the ATM
- Ann walked to the bank, and unpacked her fishing rod

It's perhaps only after reading the second sentence that it occurs to you that 'bank' can mean not only 'financial institution' but also 'river bank'. And if you're honest with yourself, it's perhaps because of *two* cognitive biases: bank as building not landscape feature, and angler as man not woman.

Or take this single-word example: can you pronounce the word *moped*? In isolation there's no way of telling whether it's *mo-PED* as in 'She rode around Rome on a moped' or *mope-t* as in 'He moped around all day'. You were primed to spot a secondary meaning, so perhaps both interpretations occurred to you – but imagine a reader who isn't primed.

An oft-cited example of an incomplete (and hence ambiguous) instruction is the aircraft maintenance manual that said, 'Check undercarriage locking pin. If bent, replace.' The mechanic did indeed check the pin, found it was bent – and put it back. The plane crashed.

The remedy for eliminating hidden assumptions is to remember to tell your readers the standard 'five Ws and one H' of *who, what, when, where, why* and *how* (to which you can add *which* and *how much*).

As we saw earlier, using the active voice often helps expose a missing *who* or *what*. Another way to root out hidden assumptions is to imagine your reader asking 'Yes, but …' questions until you reach an explanation that any sensible outsider could understand. Make all your questions open (inviting multiple responses) rather than closed (eliciting only a yes/no response), by using the WH questions (*who, what, why, how*, etc).

For example, suppose you're editing a sentence such as, 'A robust valuation process must be in place and followed to minimise errors leading to incorrect results.' If you challenge each word of the text with 'Yes, but' you'll uncover the following WH questions:

- *robust* in terms of what?
- *valuation* of what?
- *process* for what?
- *in place* where?
- *followed* by whom?
- *errors* in what?
- *results* of what?

'Why?' is a particularly interesting question. As the American philosopher, writer and cognitive scientist Daniel Dennett has observed, it's ambiguous as it can mean 'How come?' (cause, ie referring to the past) or 'What for?' (intent, ie looking towards the future). For example:

Q: *'Why do you have a risk management framework?'*

A: 'Because the chief risk officer asked us to create one' (cause) / 'To manage our risks effectively' (intent)

The better your questions, the better the answers. Or, to quote the management guru Peter Drucker, 'the most serious mistakes are not made as a result of wrong answers. The truly dangerous thing is asking the wrong question.' The more you keep challenging your own text, rooting out your hidden assumptions, the better your text will become. The same goes for editing other people's text.

A further technique for rooting out hidden assumptions is to ask yourself whether anything is obvious, cut it if it is, and see what's missing. For example, suppose you have to edit this sentence:

> We will organise a workshop for relevant participants

Your thinking goes like this:

1. Would anyone invite *irrelevant* participants? No, so I can cut the word *relevant*:

   We will organise a workshop for participants

2. Or organise a workshop without participants? Obviously not, so I can cut *for participants*:

   We will organise a workshop

3. And bingo! There it is, the hidden assumption – who's the workshop for?

Make abstract nouns concrete

A noun is 'concrete' if it describes something you can experience in the real world (*dog, bicycle, sunshine*) and 'abstract' if it describes an idea or concept (*process, freedom, belief*). This very intangibility means that abstract nouns are often drained of meaning or wide open to interpretation: a linguistic loophole cynically exploited by politicians when they use phrases such as 'family values'.

In business writing, the three most common abstract nouns are usually *process*, *procedure* and *framework*. Take a sentence such as 'A framework needs to be created.' It sounds as if it's saying something, but if you tap it for meaning you'll get nothing but an empty clang. In fact, it's worse than empty: it's sort of saying 'Someone needs to decide how to do this' (which is already empty of information) but compounding its vacuity by being written in the passive, which sucks out even the idea that anyone needs to create it.

As well as being empty, sentences with abstract nouns are often tautological. Writing 'Client acceptance testing is the process for testing software to ensure that it is acceptable to the client' is like saying 'Omelette-making is the process by which omelettes are made.'

Another problem with abstract nouns is that you often end up describing a *thing* (eg risk framework), which distracts you from explaining what you actually *do* (eg manage risks):

✗ The risk-management framework consists of …
✓ We manage our risks by …

This, then, is the fix: turn abstractions into actions. Rather than describing a concept, say what you *do*.

Fix syntactic problems (word order)

Amphibology (or amphiboly) might sound like the study of frogs, newts and other amphibians. But what it actually means is syntactic ambiguity, namely ambiguity caused by how a sentence is put together; just as a frog can breathe water *and* air, so an amphibolic sentence can be read as meaning this *and* that.

A neat example is 'Save soap and waste paper'. The fix in this case is either to rewrite waste paper as one word or reorder the words:

? Save soap and waste paper
✓ Save soap and wastepaper
✓ Save waste paper and soap

You can fix syntactic ambiguity by reordering or rewriting the sentence, or by repunctuating – typically by adding commas or hyphens to clarify what belongs to what:

- Defining governance and risk controls

  ? Defining [governance] and [risk controls]
  ? Defining [governance and risk] controls

? Defining [governance *controls*] and [risk controls]

First meaning:

✓ Defining governance, and risk controls *[added comma]*
✓ Defining risk controls and governance *[reordered words]*

Second meaning:

✓ Defining risk-and-governance controls *[added hyphens]*
✓ Defining a set of controls covering risk and governance *[rewritten]*

Third meaning:

✓ Defining one set of controls for risk and another for governance *[rewritten]*

A specific (and common) form of syntactic ambiguity is what are called 'squinting modifiers', namely words that can be read as applying to either the word before or after them. Take the word 'often' in the following example:

✗ Code that is not tested often contains bugs

? [Code that is not tested often] contains bugs
? [Code that is not tested] often contains bugs

Unlike in the earlier examples, repunctuating or flipping the word order can't save you here. Your best option is to rewrite the sentence to clarify which meaning you intend:

✓ Code that is infrequently tested contains bugs
✓ Untested code often contains bugs

Another (slightly less elegant) option for the example above is to add a word whose grammatical function is unambiguous

✓ Code that is not tested often *will* contain bugs
✓ Code that is not tested *will* often contain bugs

… bearing in mind that adding *will* means you need to drop the *-s* from *contains*.

The adverb *only* is a notorious 'squinter' so place it carefully, ideally right in front of the word it modifies. For example, 'I only edited documents' means 'The only thing I did with documents was edit them – I didn't write them' whereas if you shift *only* to come after edited ('I edited only documents') what you're now saying is 'The only things I edited were documents. Not slideshows, not web text – just documents.'

Here are some more examples of how changes in word order can subtly change your meaning. Compare:

- She sat next to him on the sofa *[two people sitting together on a sofa]*
- She sat on the sofa next to him *[he's next to a sofa on which she alone is sitting]*
- Sitting still on a chair *[sitting on a chair and not moving]*
- Still sitting on a chair *[continuing to sit on a chair]*

? Sitting on a chair *still*

The important thing is to keep words together when they form a semantic unit (chunk of meaning). Take this distracting sentence I read in an otherwise very entertaining and informative book:

? The first bumblebee was recorded in Tasmania in 1992

What's wrong with it? Well, the way the words are arranged means we mentally slice it into the following chunks:

? [The first bumblebee] [was recorded in Tasmania in 1992]

Read this way, the sentence seems to be saying the first bumblebee *ever* wasn't observed until the late twentieth century. Realising that this interpretation is absurd, we're forced (as I was) to reread the sentence to piece together the intended meaning:

✓ A bumblebee was first found in Tasmania in 1992

Carelessly ordered words can leave readers puzzling over what point you're trying to make. Take this puzzling sentence I read in a business book:

? In 2009, only 35 takeover deals worth more than $1 billion took place in the USA.

Is it saying that 35 such deals is a surprisingly low number for the whole of the United States (what the writer probably meant to say)? Or is it saying that while 35 such deals were in the United States, there were many more elsewhere in the world (the interpretation implied by the word order)?

If the first interpretation's correct, you can clarify the meaning by moving 'in the USA' to the front of the sentence, where it belongs:

✓ *In the USA* in 2009, there were only 35 takeover deals worth more than $1 billion.

If the second interpretation's correct, you can fix the sentence by keeping the original word order but appending the implied information for clarification:

✓ In 2009, only 35 takeover deals worth more than $1 billion took place in the USA – *whereas in <countries X, Y and Z> the number was <whatever>*

Word order's especially critical when you're describing anything sequential: just compare 'Check your parachute then jump' with 'Jump then check your parachute.' Similarly:

1 Delete the counterparty.
Before you do this, check you have no open trades against the counterparty.

Whoops!

Less dangerous than instructions before warnings (but still frustrating for readers) are instructions that force you to read backwards:

✗ Select **Base Currency** from the **Currencies** dropdown in the **Reference Data** menu.
✓ Select **Reference Data** > **Currencies** > **Base Currency**.

Another common instance of back-to-front instructions is putting methods before needs, as is usually the case with instructions that include the word 'allows' or 'enables'. For example, you'd never say '*A knife allows you to cut food*' (how generous of that knife to let you do this!) but '*To cut your food, use a knife*' – a human need logically precedes the thing designed to solve it. Similarly:

✗ The Search field at the top of the screen allows you to jump to a setting.
✓ To jump to a setting, use the Search field at the top of the screen.

Finally, be aware that word order can also change a sentence's connotation, as in the following sentences where the only difference is that the two clauses have swapped places:

- Our European sales are proving resilient, but the UK is still in recession and the euro crisis persists *[Cautionary tone, the message being 'We've done well so far – but we still have problems ahead']*
- The UK is still in recession and the euro crisis persists, but our European sales are proving resilient *[Congratulatory tone, the message being 'Despite significant problems, we're continuing to do well']*

Fix flawed thinking

Be vigilant against flawed thinking, because it can be very easy to overlook:

✗ Passwords must be changed *at a minimum every 90 days*

At first glance this instruction might make sense, but the author's confused stringency (minimum requirement) with frequency (minimum number of days) and hence implied that the password must be changed every 90 days or *more* – the opposite of what is meant:

✓ Passwords must be changed *every 90 days or more frequently*

Or how about this next example, 'The software needs to anticipate business changes'? You get the gist of what the writer was trying to say – that the software needs to be flexible – but the statement's nonsensical because only human beings can 'anticipate business changes', not software.

You can also risk nonsense by mixing metaphors and other figures of speech, eg 'seamlessly connected solutions' could create the surreal image of liquids being stitched together. And how about the news presenter who said that a man who'd been struck by lightning had been taken to hospital, '... and was later discharged' or the spokesperson for a flood helpline who said they'd been, '... inundated with calls'?

Another cause of unintentional humour is misplacing the pronoun 'it' – readers will assume that the noun being replaced is the one just before 'it', so that's where it needs to go. For example:

✗ He took an apple from the basket then ate it *[ate the basket?]*
✓ Reaching inside the basket he took an apple then ate it

Make sure that comparatives compare

Comparatives are words comparing one thing with another (*better*, *worse*, *higher*) and superlatives are words showing what's ultimate (*best*, *worst*, *highest*). Superlatives don't need to state a comparison, eg 'Mount Everest is the world's highest mountain' is a complete statement. But comparatives do: the clue's in the name. For example, if I tell you 'An elephant's bigger' you're left wondering, 'Bigger than *what*?' As well as being confusing, incomplete comparatives can be downright dishonest, as in those sneaky adverts that say things such as, 'A new toothbrush cleans 95% better' – better than *what*? A week-old toothbrush? Not cleaning your teeth at all?

So if you have a comparative, make sure you explain what it's being compared with:

✗ The relationship between longevity and default risks is less defined *[than what?]*

✓ The relationship between longevity and default risks is less defined *than that between other risk drivers in the model*

Remove tautologies

Look for circular statements. Here's a genuine example from marketing copy I edited:

> How do we support operational business requirements? Our enterprise risk management (ERM) services include advice on optimal processes and committees needed to support ERM. In this way we inherently look to support our clients' operational business requirements.

Since ERM *is* processes overseen by committees, writing the above is tantamount to saying, 'We support your requirements by advising on the best way to meet your requirements. This is how we support your requirements.'

What you need instead is something such as:

> We will advise you on all aspects of enterprise risk management (ERM), from identifying and mitigating risks, to optimising your business processes, to determining the governance structure you need.

Avoid negatives, especially the word 'not'

Negative statements, especially those created using the word 'not', can cause several problems. First, 'not' can make reading harder, especially when it's far from the word it negates:

✗ The report *does not* contain *sufficient* information

✓ The report contains *insufficient* information

Particularly hard to understand are multiple negatives. Even Alexander the Great would struggle to cut through a Gordian knot of 'not nots' such as the following:

✗ It's not that I never don't use negatives

Here's another problem with 'not'. If someone says to you, 'Do *not* think of a white bear,' what does your brain do? The opposite! It's called 'the white bear problem' or 'ironic process theory' and, since people struggle to process negative statements, use positive ones instead:

✗ Do not *eat unhealthy food*
✓ *Eat healthy food*

The white bear problem affects not only people's immediate comprehension but also what they remember. I once worked on a project to overhaul the website for the Open University, where we tested readers' comprehension by asking them what they remembered. One statement was, 'The Open University does *not* have a campus, but it does have an administrative centre in Milton Keynes.' When later asked what they remembered our readers replied, 'The OU has a campus in Milton Keynes.'

A similar remembering-the-wrong-thing problem can occur if you tell people something from your perspective rather than theirs. I once told a recruitment firm that my last day in my current contract (my viewpoint) was 14 May instead of the first date I could start my next contract (their viewpoint), namely the day after. When they later asked me to confirm my start date, guess what date they remembered? Yep – the date I'd told them, not the unstated date they had to infer.

Incidentally, the white bear problem is so cognitively powerful that sneaky salespeople will often use it to bypass people's buying objections by embedding unconscious commands, a technique called reverse psychology. For example:

- I'm *not* going to tell you to *buy this product* until you *hear all the facts*

Another problem with 'not' is ambiguity. If you say what something is *not* you're leaving wide open to interpretation what it *is*. For example, 'This is not a good choice' leaves people wondering, 'What *is* a good choice then?' Similarly, [not + noun] constructions can introduce ambiguities eliminated by replacing the 'not' with a prefix or different word:

? This person is not professional *[amateur or incompetent?]*
✓ This person is a non-professional / amateur / hobbyist
✓ This person is unprofessional

Also, avoid ambiguities caused by 'negative raising', which is when a *not* shifts from the thing it logically negates to a preceding verb (such as *think* or *believe*). In *Metaphors We Live By*, George Lakoff and Mark Johnson give the following example:

> Mary thinks he *won't* leave until tomorrow
> (raised) Mary *doesn't* think he'll leave until tomorrow

In the above example, it's fairly clear that the two sentences are equivalent. But consider the following example:

? We don't believe the results are accurate

Which leaves readers wondering which of the following you mean:

✓ We are unsure if the results are accurate
✓ We believe that the results are inaccurate

Notice too the subtle benefit of *that* in the second example: although 'We believe the results are inaccurate' wouldn't be wrong, it would be easy to misread because the first four words ('We believe the results') read like a full sentence saying the opposite of what you mean.

Another linguistic snare caused by 'not' is due to the fact that English is limited to only two words for answering in the affirmative and negative, namely 'yes' and 'no' (what's called a two-form system). This limitation means that negatively posed questions can lead to ambiguous answers. Take a question such as 'You're not good at your job, are you?' If your only possible responses are 'yes' and 'no' you're trapped whatever you say:

- If you answer 'yes', listeners wonder whether you're saying:

  ? 'Yes, you're right – I'm not good at my job' [agreement]
  ? 'Yes, I bloody well am good at my job!' [disagreement]

- But if you answer 'no', they're left torn between:

  ? 'No, I'm not good at my job, am I?' [agreement]
  ? 'No, that's wrong – I am good at my job!' [disagreement]

Such ambiguities are avoided in languages with a three-form system, such as French (*oui*, *non*, *si*) and German (*ja*, *nein*, *doch*) where *si* and *doch* are clear denials (equivalent, in the examples above, to simultaneously saying 'Yes, I bloody well am!' and 'No, that's wrong').

But since English doesn't have the linguistic luxury of a three-form system, it's best to avoid negatively posed questions to avoid provoking replies that need qualification to be understood.

The final reasons for avoiding 'not' are that it can cause a disagreeable tone and it's often bad psychology. Compare the childish whine of *It's not fair* with the grown-up tone of *It's unfair*, and how *It's not unreasonable to expect* sounds weak and evasive but *I expect* sounds assertive. And imagine if instead of 'I'm not a crook' Richard Nixon had said 'I'm an honest man' – it would still have been a lie, but would it have damaged him quite as much as what he actually said?

Any [not + negative word] construction is usually bad psychology, because to our unconscious the 'not' reinforces rather than cancels the negative message, ie negative + negative = very negative. Imagine, for example, you've just been on a first date. How would your feelings change if your date said the following words in italics or left them out?

> *Don't get me wrong*; I really like you. *Please do not hesitate to* call me!

For this reason, always avoid the expression 'Please do not hesitate to'. Its obvious sin is that it's a cliché and verbose; its less obvious sin is that it's bad psychology. Avoid using [not + negative word] even for deliberate ironic understatement, as in the phrase 'Not bad!' This rhetorical device might have the fancy Greek name of 'litotes' but it's the opposite of persuasive. For example, suppose you ask someone if they're feeling good. Will you believe they're happy if they reply, 'Not bad, can't complain, mustn't grumble'? Or imagine how you'd feel if you've just shaken hands on a deal to buy a second-hand car and the salesperson says, 'You won't be sorry!'

Avoid jargon

Avoid jargon, as it's often confusing to outsiders and ambiguous even to insiders. I'm not talking about technical vocabulary, such as my earlier example of a heart surgeon using the phrase 'myocardial infarction' if writing for a medical audience but 'heart attack' if writing for the public. What I'm talking about instead is insider words when ordinary words suffice.

One team I worked for illogically referred to deliverables (even non-physical ones such as new processes) as 'products' while another referred to documents as 'artefacts' – which not only obscured what they actually were but also made them sound like something from ancient history or a crime scene (but considering how some were written, maybe they were).

Jargon can be seductive because it marks you as an insider – but always remember that writing isn't about you but about your readers. We can all laugh at wine snobs who try to hide the banality of saying 'it smells and tastes good' by confusing the wine with the drinker ('This burgundy has a good nose and is drinking well'), but watch out for equally absurd jargon in your own writing, such as the following:

- *Granular* instead of *detailed*: The word 'granular' is doubly ridiculous because (a) it's used as the opposite of its synonym 'grainy' and (b) saying that something is *more granular* is like saying that a hot day is *more temperatured* than a cold day: what the metaphor demands is *finely grained* v *coarsely grained*. Also, *granular* can be ambiguous: for example, does the phrase 'high level of granularity' mean 'highly granular' (ie fine-grained) or 'granularity at a high level' (ie coarse-grained)?
- *Box* instead of *server*: What, you mean a cardboard box? A TV? Unlike technical words such as *blade* or *mainframe* (which add precision), *box* used instead of *server* obscures meaning.
- *Space* instead of *business sector*: The word 'space' is both a cliché and imprecise. It can also be unintentionally comical, as in 'Customer relationships are under attack in the retail space' – a genuine example from text I was given to edit that sounds less like commercial pressure on the retail sector than fisticuffs in a shop.

Future-proof your text

A statement such as 'I've been a writer for thirty years' is true only for the year in which it's written, but 'My career began in 1989' remains forever true. So for any text intended to be durable it's wise to future-proof it by replacing relative dates and times with ones that are absolute: hence not 'this year' but 'in 2021', not 'last month' but 'in November'.

To make your text eternal, consider replacing date-time information altogether. A statement such as 'Colours popular in the autumn of 2015' is meaningless if future readers don't remember (or care) what colours were popular then – whereas 'the autumn colours russet and cinnamon' is immediately meaningful no matter how far into the future the text is read.

What if you're describing something that's in the future at the time of writing, but will be current when the document's published? Do you write 'will' (true now, but risky because you might forget to update it) or 'is' (true at publication time, but could be misleading if read now)? Sometimes you can write round the problem, as I once did with the following edit to a document to be submitted to a financial regulator:

- This is the entity ~~that will~~ <u>*designated to*</u> hold the capital requirement for the pension scheme

Anticipate and rebut objections

If you're expecting objections to what you've said, a clever trick is to acknowledge those objections then rebut them – a trick so old that Greek rhetoricians had a name for it, *prolepsis* (or, if you want a more modern name, prebuttal). For example:

✓ If you're thinking our software seems expensive, you're right. In fact, our licensing fees are nearly twice as high as those of our nearest rivals. But what they won't tell you is that our software runs three times as fast as theirs and generates four times as many leads. And we don't have any hidden consultancy fees.

✓ The exec committee suggested that closing the Bristol office and offshoring our support centre is the obvious way to cut costs. But as you may recall from our disastrous closure of the Glasgow office last year, offshoring creates unforeseen problems and – ultimately – costs more money.

Tell people what they need to do

If what you've written is meant to get people to act, you need a 'call to action' – a clear statement of what you want them to do and *how*. The *how* bit's essential – for instance, a call to action asking people to phone you will fail if you forget to give them your number! Here are some effective calls to action, with explanations as to why they work:

✓ To book your appointment, call **now** on (0800) xxx xxxx

As well as having the two essential ingredients of *what* and *how*, this call to action creates a sense of urgency by using the word *now*.

Remember that whatever medium your message appears in, people can always leave without acting: they can turn the page, click the next link, hit Delete. Even if they intend to return later, chances are they won't. Just think of your own 'I'll read them later' emails and articles – did you revisit them or forget them instead? The lesson? Do everything you can to get people to act on your message *now*.

A further and subtler reason that this call to action is effective is that it says '*your* appointment' rather than '*an* appointment' – subtly suggesting to readers that they've already agreed to see you.

✓ **Go to training** (button on a website)

This call to action neither explicitly tells people *how* nor insists they do it *now* – yet it works. Why? Because both missing elements are implicit: the 'how' in that it's a button that's meant to be clicked, and the 'now' because the button's right there, right now – so if as a reader I'm interested in training I'll click.

Also, the button label is informative and contains a verb (ie an action): readers know exactly where they'll be taken when they click. As Ginny Redish points out in *Letting Go of the Words: Writing Web Content that Works*, blind people often skim websites using screen-reading software that lists all of a website's links – so it's essential to avoid button labels that repeat phrases that depend on context to be understood, phrases such as **Learn more** and **Click here**.

What applies to buttons applies to URL text as well.

✓ Download our free investment guide or sign up to our newsletter

Offering two choices increases the likelihood that your readers will act, as does giving a closed choice between two options that force a 'yes'. As a further example of the effectiveness of a closed choice, compare these two questions:

- 'Do you want to meet today?' leaves open the option to say no
- 'Do you want to meet this morning or this afternoon?' implies that we *will* meet today, it's just a question of when

Calls to action are essential on any sales literature. That includes business websites, which are essentially shops (what's their point if they don't generate business?) – so every page on your firm's public website needs to steer visitors, as fast and persuasively as possible, from the window to the counter.

And don't overlook calls to action in more everyday material. Even an email asking people to confirm their attendance at Tuesday's team meeting needs to state clearly what recipients need to do and how.

Fix weasel words and hedging

Weasel words are words used to fudge details or even mislead people. Remove them, and make explicit what was being glossed over:

✗ Up to 20% faster across all browsers
✓ 20% faster on Chrome, 17% faster on Firefox and 15% faster on Safari
✗ This is probably the best option, and should give the best performance
✓ We recommend option 2, as it has consistently outperformed the others

Make overgeneralisations precise

Overgeneralisations expose lazy thinking, fail to inform readers of anything meaningful, and usually state the obvious. They're especially lethal in case studies and other marketing material when clumsily used to shoehorn in a pitch. Here are a couple of examples, along with the sorts of thoughts they might generate in readers:

✗ In today's fast-moving world, companies are struggling to meet the challenges of … The solution is our leading-edge cyber product …

['Fast-moving' in terms of what? Which companies? Why are they struggling? And hang on – you're pitching me your product as a 'solution' when you haven't even explained the problem?!]

✗ In the past, bank customers had to …

['In the past' relative to what? How long ago: last century, last five years, two months ago, last week? What's changed now? Why?]

✗ To succeed, companies must move towards a customer-centric model.

[What, succeeding in business depends on meeting customers' needs? You don't say!]

You've two options for fixing over-generalisations. The first fix is to give specifics, thereby making your sales pitch credible:

✗ In the past, bank customers had to …
✓ January 2018 was a watershed date for UK banking customers as significant as June 1967, when the UK's first ever ATM went into operation. Why? Because a UK ruling forced the UK's nine biggest banks to share their data with licensed Open Banking start-ups – meaning a surge in mobile apps that enable customers to …

Changing generalities to specifics requires more effort, that's true. But lazy sales writing means disengaged customers, the very people who'll write something important to *you*: your paycheque.

And the second fix? Wield your editorial scalpel and simply cut the offending sentences. Removing non-statements such as 'To succeed, companies must move towards a customer-centric model' won't kill your prose but cure it.

Use words consistently and precisely

Avoid using the same term for different things, or different terms for the same thing. I remember being flummoxed by a document that referred to both *attribution* and *allocation*, until someone told me they meant the same thing. Glossaries can be invaluable for clarifying terms and avoiding misunderstandings.

Similarly, replace words with multiple meanings with ones that are unambiguous:

? *Lower* costs
✓ *Reduced* / *Reduce* costs
? Meetings are *bimonthly*
✓ Meetings are *fortnightly* / *every two months*
? *While* I worked there, I didn't know him
✓ *When* / *Although* I worked there, I didn't know him

Here's another example, this one requiring more than just a word change:

✗ Execute permissions unnecessary for the service functionality must be removed

Did you misread that 'Execute' at the start as a verb, then get thrown by the real verb tucked away at the end of the sentence?

✓ Remove unnecessary 'execute' permissions

Sentences that trip you up like this are known as 'garden-path sentences', so called because they lead you up the garden path into a false reading – like this gem:

> Time flies like an arrow; fruit flies like a banana.

In such situations where a noun can be misread as a verb (or vice versa), one fix is adding an article (*a*, *an* or *the*):

? It may require manipulation to model outputs

- ✓ (*verb*) … to model *the* outputs
- ✓ (*noun*) … to *the* model outputs
- ✓ (*noun, eliminating singular/plural ambiguity*) … to *the* model'*s*/ model*s'* outputs

Handle problem words carefully

Avoid (or at least handle carefully) the following words, as they often cause problems.

Appropriate, relevant

Appropriate and *relevant* are depressingly common clichés in bad business writing, both being misused as catchall words for anything vaguely positive. There's no point in saying something's 'appropriate' or 'relevant' unless you explain what they're appropriate or relevant *for*. Pick the word that best matches the meaning you intended:

✓ The approach is ~~appropriate~~ *[the most reliable / complies with regulations / proportionate]*

But

If you intend to contrast two ideas, *but* is often the best word to use:

✓ Losing your temper can feel good, *but* it can harm a business relationship

But it's this very ability to contrast ideas that can make *but* a risky word to use. Take this example:

✗ I hear what you're saying, *but* …

If anyone's ever said this to you, you'll know how frustrating it is to hear because you know that it actually means 'but I'm not listening.' As Roger Fisher and William Ury explain in their book *Getting to Yes – Negotiating an Agreement Without Giving In*, the word *but* is sometimes called the 'great eraser' because it, '… has the tendency to negate the first thing you say by implying that only one of two statements can be true, making it either/or.' When you want to avoid the either/or, use *and* instead:

✓ I hear what you're saying, *and* …

Cover

Ambiguous when misused as a vague catchall verb:

✗ The tests are *covered by* the calibrations documents, and testing requirements are *covered by* the data governance standard
✓ The tests are *described in* the calibrations documents, and testing requirements are *specified in* the data governance standard

Ensure, assure, think, believe, etc (verbs missing 'that')

In corporate writing, many verbs (especially *ensure*) are often written without *that* when adding *that* would have removed an ambiguity. For example, try making sense of this sentence with and without *that*:

? The horse raced past the barn fell
✓ The horse *that* raced past the barn fell

Similarly, notice how a missing 'that' in the following sentence leads readers up a garden path, forcing them to reread the whole thing to make sense of it:

? We insure the board receives regular reports *['We provide insurance to the board … receives regular reports' – huh?]*
✓ We insure *that* the board receives regular reports

Even better, change *insure* (which has two meanings) to *ensure* (which has only one):

✓ We *ensure that* the board receives regular reports

Facilitate

Potentially a weasel word because it can fudge responsibility:

✗ The account manager *facilitates [helps with / conducts?]* the negotiations

Fit for purpose

A weasel phrase, because it evades explaining what something is suitable *for*:

✗ The user interface must be *fit for purpose [which purposes?]*
✓ The user interface must *run on all standard browsers, mobile devices …*

I, we

Like other pronouns, 'I' and 'we' cause problems when it's unclear who's being referred to. Suppose the original author writes 'I did this, I did that' – the moment someone else edits the document, it's no longer clear who 'I' is.

'We' can be ambiguous, because English (like most European languages) lacks clusivity, meaning it can't distinguish between 'inclusive we' ('you and me') and 'exclusive we' ('me and someone other than the person I'm addressing').

To use an example given by the YouTuber Tom Scott, imagine a group of friends talking and one says to the other, 'We've just won the lottery!'

- Inclusive we: The person being addressed is in luck because the speaker's saying, 'We, that's to say you and I, have won the lottery!'
- Exclusive we: The addressee is out of luck because the speaker's saying, 'We, that's to say my friends and I, have won the lottery. *You* haven't!'

You can sense this ambiguity in the frequent urge people feel to put 'together' in front of 'we', as in this advert from Cancer UK:

> Together we can beat cancer

Imagine it without 'Together' and it feels like Cancer UK congratulating themselves on their ability to fight cancer. With it, it's like Lord Kitchener's finger pointing out from that famous conscription poster saying, 'Your country needs you' – '*Together* (that's us and *you*) we can beat cancer.'

Similarly, consider the 'together or alone?' ambiguity if someone from HR wrote the following statement:

? HR and Finance discussed staff layoffs proposed by the board. We agreed with the proposals.

Does it mean 'HR, amongst ourselves, agreed with the board's proposals (but Finance may or may not have)' or does it mean 'Finance and HR jointly agreed with the board's proposals'?

Materially

The word 'materially' is often used where it's either irrelevant or unquantified:

? The basis used has a *material* impact on the results

Either quantify the materiality (if materiality is important) or don't mention it at all (if it's beside the point):

✓ The basis used affects the results *by up to 5%, a level considered material*
✓ The basis used affects the results

The next example shows someone using 'materially' to mislead, by trying to hint that work has started when patently it hasn't, then lying about non-existent 'reasons':

✗ The data migration has not *materially* started (*due to various reasons*)

State the truth, elaborating with details and reasons if you feel them necessary. People will respect you if you do:

✓ The data migration has not started
✓ The data migration has not started, because *[specific reasons]*
✓ The team has written a scope document, but not yet migrated any data

May

Ambiguous when it's unclear if permission or possibility is meant:

✗ Sample reports *may* include real data
✓ Sample reports *are allowed to / might* include real data

Also avoid using *may* as a weasel word to distance yourself from responsibility, as in train announcements such as this one:

✗ The 17:40 train to Victoria has been cancelled. We apologise *for any inconvenience this may cause you.*

Onerous

Avoid the word 'onerous' unless you're using it in a precise technical sense (such as an annuity being 'onerous' if it costs the pension provider more than it accrues). Why? Because its more common meaning is 'effortful or troublesome', which merely says how you feel about a problem rather than explaining it.

For example, saying a calculation is onerous leaves readers wondering why: because it's computationally demanding, complex to analyse, expensive to develop, something else? Whenever you need precision rather than opinion, always replace judgemental words with factual ones. This point's really important, so we'll be looking at it in depth later on.

Paper

The word *paper* (weirdly common in corporate writing) suggests an academic report or essay: use a more suitable and accurate word such as *report, proposal, policy* or *guide.*

Robust

Like 'appropriate' in that it's often misused as a catchall word, approximating to 'good'. As with 'appropriate', the solution is to pick the most precise word you can, such as *reliable*, *verifiable* or *quantifiable*.

Should, could, would, ought

All these words suggest doubt: *must*, *can* and *will* are usually preferable. The word *should* has the further disadvantage of often being ambiguous:

✗ The project scope *should be [is likely to be / must be?]* specified in the client contract.

And please don't write *should* when you mean *if*, unless you want to sound like a butler:

✗ Should you wish to partake of a cup of tea
✓ If you'd like a cup of tea

System, application, etc

When naming something, avoid generic terms such as *system*, *application* and *user*:

✗ The *module's columns* are refreshed after the *service* has initialised
✓ The *details of today's trades* are refreshed after the *blotter service* has initialised

Why? Because often the text is referring to several systems (or applications, types of user, or whatever), and it's not always obvious from the context which one.

Take into account

Often ambiguous – replace it with a more precise word:

✗ The internal model must *take into account* new information
✓ The internal model must *consider / adapt to / incorporate* new information

This, these

Both *this* and *these* cause problems if what they're referring to (the 'referent') is ambiguous. Even when the referent isn't ambiguous, the reader's often forced to backtrack through the preceding text to remember or puzzle out what on earth the referent is. Either add the referent ('this *whatever*') or trim the problem words:

- ✗ Evidence needs to be collated centrally. *This* will become key next year.
- ✓ (*add referent*) Evidence needs to be collated centrally. This *requirement* will become key next year.
- ✓ (*cut 'This'*) Evidence needs to be collated centrally, by next year.

A common failing is *this* or *these* whose referent is stranded in the previous paragraph. Remove the paragraph break (and trim *this/these* if possible):

- ✗ Next we set the dependency structure between risk factors.
  This is done using a copula structure.
- ✓ Next we set the dependency structure between risk factors, using a copula structure.

Often, *this/these* is used where *it/them* would be better:

- ✓ The payments are fairly predictable, reducing the need to cover ~~these~~ *them*.

TRIM VERBOSITY AND CLICHÉS

In this step we're going to trim any fat. Or, to use another analogy from cookery, we're going to reduce our verbiage like a chef reduces a sauce: boiling off the watery words to intensify the flavour and thicken the impact. Then we're going to make our words even tastier by replacing anything stale (such as clichés) with fresher ingredients.

Syntactic expletives

Despite their risqué-sounding name, syntactic expletives aren't rude words. Instead, they're words that make a sentence function grammatically but add no meaning. They clog your prose, so cut them wherever you can:

- Megasoft's proposal employs principles ~~that are~~ derived from similar projects
- calibration ~~of the~~ risk > risk calibration

Note that if you're using Microsoft Word you can find and replace – in one search – all instances of the '*<noun 2> of the <noun 1>*' pattern with '*<noun 1> <noun 2>*'. Word's help explains how.

A final word on syntactic expletives – do your best to eradicate the deathly phrases '*There is*' and '*There are*', especially at the start of sentences. First, they make everything feel reported rather than experienced. Feel how much more energetic your prose feels without them:

✗ There is a dog jumping over the fence
✓ A dog jumps over the fence

Second, as Yellowlees Douglas explains in *The Reader's Brain: How Neuroscience Can Make You a Better Writer*, 'There is' displaces the true subject of the sentence (*The dog*) with a vacuous adverb (*There*) and displaces an action verb (*jumps*) with a non-action verb (*is*), '… which really jams your readers' radar'.

Even where there's no action, sentences read better if you can chop out *There is/are*. Compare:

✗ There is a separate server for each database
✓ Each server has a separate database

Remember also *there is/are* equivalents in other tenses, such as *there was/were, there will be, there would have been*, and so on. In fact, one great way to make life easier for yourself (and your readers) is to find and replace every single *there*: unless it's functioning as in 'here and there' you can probably do without it.

Nouns that repeat verbs and other nouns

Delete nouns that repeat a verb, be it literally or implicitly:

- Living ~~*our lives*~~ in peace
- He heard ~~*a*~~ scratching ~~*sound*~~

And do the same for nouns repeating nouns:

- In ~~*the month of*~~ May
- In two weeks ~~*time*~~
- Under two miles ~~*distance*~~ from here

Redundant adjectives and adverbs

Delete all adjectives inherent in their nouns. For example:

- Creating ~~*new*~~ or modifying ~~*existing*~~ entities (you can't create something old, nor can you modify something that doesn't exist)
- ~~*Separate*~~ components (components are, by definition, separate)

- ~~Potential~~ risk (if it were actualised, it wouldn't be a risk)
- ~~Current~~ status (redundant if status is used in the sense of 'current situation')
- ~~Advanced~~ warning (how could it be a warning otherwise?)
- Your ~~personal~~ belongings (if they're yours, they're yours)
- ~~Oven-baked~~ bread (as opposed to dishwasher-baked bread? And if not baked, it would be 'dough'. Compare with *crusty*, *rye* and *sourdough*, justified because they add meaning not contained in the noun)

Similarly, delete adverbs implicit from their verbs, eg shout ~~loudly~~, focus ~~primarily~~, and ~~clearly~~ explain.

TLA redundancy

We've looked at redundant modifiers that are words. Harder to spot and therefore more insidious are modifiers disguised as letters in TLAs, namely three-letter abbreviations.

One that I commonly encounter is 'SMEs' for subject-matter experts. Writers get so familiar with the term that every time they could write *expert* they feel the need to tag on *subject-matter* – which is stupid, because an expert is, by definition, someone who knows about their subject matter. Even *subject matter* is stupid, because a subject is, well, a subject, and doesn't need the useless appendage *matter*. And 'SME' can also stand for 'small to medium enterprise' so it's confusing as well as silly to use it where *expert* will do.

Many TLAs are hard to avoid. But once in a while it's worth unpacking them to see if there's a single, everyday word lurking inside that you can use instead.

Redundant prefixes

Avoid *pre-* where it's not needed or introduces absurdity. For example, ~~pre~~warn (warn already contains the idea of 'coming before'), *pre*book (ditto) and the particularly absurd ~~pre~~-prepare.

Clichéd adjectives

Some adjective-noun formations are so clichéd that the adjective is all but redundant: hills do not always need to be 'rolling', nor ranks 'serried' nor the public 'general'.

Clichéd pairings such as these are known as collocations and even professional writers fall into the trap of using them. Pick up any crime novel and read the blurb on the back: 99 times out of a 100, a murder will be described as 'brutal'. What murder isn't? And isn't it more fascinating or terrifying if it's *unexplained*, *sinister* or *slow*? The same principle applies, of course, to adverbial collocations: ~~*brutally*~~ murdered, and so on.

In a business context you're unlikely to be discussing a '~~*brutal*~~ murder' (although an obnoxious boss or awkward customer might warrant it) – but if you feel the urge to automatically qualify a noun/verb with the first adjective/adverb that comes to mind, take a ~~*long, hard*~~ look at the offending words and ~~*brutally*~~ murder them.

Imprecise nouns requiring adjectives

Replace any [adjective + imprecise noun] with a more precise noun, often the noun from which the adjective is derived:

- shopping facilities > shops
- regulatory requirements > regulations
- email communications > emails
- contractual agreements > contracts
- underwriting function > underwriters

That last example, the [job role + function] construction, infests corporate writing and you can nearly always simplify it to [job role], for instance *risk function* > *risk managers*, *legal function* > *lawyers*, and *actuarial function* > *actuaries*. Similarly, *senior member of the actuarial team* > *senior actuary*.

Sometimes you can simply cut the offending word:

- reporting ~~arrangements~~
- weather ~~conditions~~

… or even replace an entire abstract phrase with a single precise noun:

- ~~adverse weather conditions~~ > snow

Imprecise verbs requiring adverbs

Just as you can replace [adjective + imprecise noun] with a more precise noun, so you can replace [adverb + imprecise verb] with a more precise verb:

- adversely affect > harm / damage / hurt

Notice too that while *harm* improves on *adversely affect* in being more concise, *damage* and *hurt* are even better because they differentiate between harm to a thing (damage) and harm to a sentient animal (hurt).

As well as making your meaning clearer, precise verbs make your writing more vivid. Compare, for example, *walk slowly* with *limp*, *stagger*, *crawl* and *amble*; and *walk fast* with *hurry*, *march*, *strut* and *stride*. Improving your diction (to use the writerly name for accurate word choice) is one of the best writing habits you can develop.

Multisyllabic words, eg -ness nouns

Watch out for long words you can shorten:

- ✗ Determining the *appropriateness* of the assumptions
- ✓ Determining if the assumptions are *appropriate*
- The method~~ology~~ used is a Gaussian copula *['methodology' means 'system of methods', so in this instance it's not only longer but also wrong]*

On rare occasions a well-placed long word can create a subtle effect. Compare:

- Complex markets require the best data tools
- Complex markets necessitate the best data tools

The four syllables of 'necessitate' force readers to brake slightly, having the same effect as italicising 'require' – namely shifting the emphasis from what markets require to the fact that the requirement is essential. It's a bit like when people say 'Abso-*lute*-ly!' if answering 'Yes' just doesn't feel emphatic enough.

But be warned: the more you overdo this trick, the less effect it has. A sentence stuffed with long words loses changes of tempo and becomes merely sluggish. In most cases, shorter is better – especially when you want readers to act:

- ✗ To guarantee a reservation on the course, it is necessary to book immediately
- ✓ Places are limited, so book now

Novelists frequently vary word and sentence length to change mood and pace. Next time you read a good novel, notice how scenes where characters are relaxed typically use languid language and long sentences. But fight scenes? Arguments? Chases? Short sentences, short words. Faster tempo.

Complex verb constructions

Complex verb constructions can be hard to understand, especially for people whose first language isn't English. So stick to the simplest verb constructions you can:

✗ These banks *would have been able to have adapted* to new markets *had* they *designed* platforms that *were* scalable.
✓ To *adapt* to new markets, these banks *needed* scalable platforms.

The following whopper is a genuine example from a document I edited:

✗ *Consider* whether to *undertake* an investigation to *assess* whether it *is* appropriate to *review* the granularity of the various assumptions for the impact on the onerousness of contracts.
… which can be trimmed to:
✓ *Check* whether detailed assumptions *make* contracts more onerous.

Also note that you can always replace *is able to* / *are able to* with *can*.

A subtle advantage of using the simplest verb form of all, especially in text designed to persuade, is that in English the infinitive of a verb (eg 'to run') is identical to the imperative or command form ('run!') – so you can embed disguised commands in your text. Compare:

- You'll be getting the best results
- You'll get the best results

Which feels more persuasive? You probably said the second version, because of the disguised command 'get the best results'.

Repeated words

Repeated words make reading harder – readers have more words to read and they're forced to concentrate on similarities rather than differences:

✗ The risks are categorised into high, medium and low materiality, which influences the frequency at which they are recalibrated. High *materiality risks are recalibrated* annually, medium *materiality risks are recalibrated* at least once every three years and low *materiality risks are recalibrated* at least once every five years.
✓ Risks judged 'high' materiality are recalibrated yearly, 'medium' within three years and 'low' within five years.

The original is *three times* as long as the rewrite (48 words to 16) – just imagine how much that sort of repetition adds up over the course of an entire document.

Repeated words plus an excess of linking words (such as *and*, *also*, *in addition to*) are often a giveaway that you can trim sentences into a list. Look at the following example, and notice how 'report describes how' occurs in all three sentences, a clear indication that the text is crying out to be a list:

> The report describes how risks are captured. The report also describes how risks are assigned to risk drivers. In addition, the report describes how risks are kept up to date in the repository.

Now look what happens when you trim the text to a list:

> The report describes how risks are: captured, assigned, and kept up to date in the repository.

In this instance, you can even dispense with the colon and turn the list into a single sentence.

Winston Churchill got away with repeated words at the start of each sentence in his famous 'We shall fight on the beaches, we shall fight on the landing grounds …' speech. But that's because he was doing it deliberately and skilfully for emphasis (a rhetorical trick called anaphora). But without a sense of rhetoric or poetry, repeated words are confusing and annoying, and so best avoided.

Hedging

Earlier we looked at weasel words, namely words used to mislead or hedge. As well as their potential for dishonesty, they can lead to waffle. Take this example from an actuarial document I once edited:

✗ An underwriting rationale, and potentially a need for more senior underwriter sign-off (subject to agreed procedures within the unit's underwriting protocols) should be stated in writing to explain the reasons for writing a risk.

This overgrown hedge is written by someone you sense really doesn't want to commit to *anything*. Trim the hedges and what you're left with is this:

✓ Underwriters must explain in writing why they are accepting a risk.

When trimming hedges, the things to look out for are:

✗ Anything that reeks of legalese, such as: notwithstanding; including (but not limited to); subject to all applicable procedures, legal constraints and regulatory requirements
✗ A tangle of subordinate clauses, parentheses and other such overgrowths blocking the view

Saying what you're saying (metadiscourse)

Another common cause of waffle is saying what you're saying, instead of just saying it. At home you'd never say (unless being facetious), 'I am proud to announce that supper's ready' – you'd just say 'Supper's ready'. Similarly, you don't need to write, 'Our company is proud to announce' when you can just announce it.

As well as being redundant, phrases such as 'We are proud to announce' are egocentric, pulling the attention away from what interests readers towards what the writer wants to boast about. Estate agents are often guilty of this mistake. Take a property listing that says something such as, 'London Properties are proud to bring to market this delightful three-bedroom flat' – the point at which the reader is interested and engaged is not until 'three-bedroom flat' (whether the flat is 'delightful' is a matter for the reader to decide from the evidence).

The redundancy of discussing what you're discussing is called 'metadiscourse' and you can nearly always cut it. Let's look at three more examples of metadiscourse.

First, writing that you're writing, eg:

✗ I am writing to you because

Second, attributing your ideas, a particularly irksome form of metadiscourse because it's often misused as a way to evade responsibility:

✗ ~~It is envisaged that~~ a new ledger system will be needed
✓ We need a new ledger system

Third, announcing your topic:

✗ ~~This procedure explains how~~ to install your upgrade

Common instances of announcing your topic in business writing are introductions explaining what tables contain (the column headings do that anyway), and chapter preambles of the form 'This chapter contains' followed by a list of section headings – a huge maintenance burden, and pointless when readers can see the headings for themselves.

Also, if chapters are well structured, each heading flows naturally from what preceded it: so feeling the need to explain what your chapter contains could indicate that your flow is incoherent. So fix the flow, then ask yourself if the metadiscourse is still needed. Probably not.

Thinking on the page

I once received an email containing two paragraphs of muddled thinking, followed by a third paragraph that started with: 'I suppose what I'm trying to say is ...' followed by a succinct explanation of what the first two paragraphs had failed to say.

'Thinking on the page' is acceptable in a first draft written for yourself – but confusing and downright rude in a draft for your readers. And it's a pain for you as well, because garbled messages (emails especially) are likely to generate garbled replies. Once a brain dump has served its purpose, remember to delete it.

Grandmothers' eggs

In honour of the phrase 'teaching your grandmother to suck eggs', let's call any explanation to readers of what they already know a *grandmother's egg*. A common example is lazy copywriting that describes an obvious need at tedious length merely to shoehorn in a pitch for a product or service, eg:

✗ In the wake of the financial crisis and ever-increasing regulations, many banks are struggling. They are looking to enhance their risk platforms.

✓ Need to enhance your risk platform?

As well as wasting words, grandmothers' eggs risk patronising your readers. I once edited a document an insurer was sending to its regulator that explained what an annuity is – which is as patronising as telling the board of CERN what an atom is.

Over-signposting

Imagine you're on the motorway, travelling at 70 miles an hour, looking for the exit for London. Which of the following signs would be more helpful?

Figure 1.4 Over-signposting

Similarly, if you're signposting in your website or document:

✗ In the event of an emergency whilst travelling, you can get assistance by visiting our travel website for information or you can call our helpline, which is open 24/7 and free to call from within the UK, on 0800 …
✓ Travelling and in trouble? Visit our travel website or call 0800 …

In other words, don't waste your reader's time and attention describing what you're pointing them towards: just briefly describe the need (why they'd want to click) and send them swiftly on their way.

Stating what's obvious or implicit

Avoid stating the obvious. Let's look at some examples.

If you're introducing a list of items you don't you don't need to state that those items exist, nor how many of them there are (readers can count), nor that they're different from each other:

✗ Other choices exist, and these fit into three categories
✓ The choices are

You don't need the irksome phrase 'Going forward' when talking of the future because forwards is the only direction in which time can travel:

✗ Going forward, the policies will apply across the whole company
✓ The policies will apply across the whole company

And talking of policies, we all know they comprise a set of terms. Therefore:

✗ You must comply with the terms of this policy
✓ You must comply with this policy

We also all know that if something occurs 'every six months' it is, by definition, 'ongoing':

✗ Ongoing reviews will be performed every six months
✓ Reviews will be every six months

When giving instructions, you don't need to say 'you can [whatever]' – it's obvious something is possible if you're explaining how to do it:

✗ You can submit a change request by clicking the Request button
✓ To submit a change request, click the Request button

Nor do you need to say that something is 'responsible for' something else when all you mean is it does it. Use the phrase 'responsible for' only when you're actually talking about responsibility:

✗ The carburettor is responsible for mixing fuel with air
✓ The carburettor mixes fuel with air
✓ The board delegates daily operations to the risk committee, but remains responsible for the company's regulatory compliance.

And to show that it's not only business writers who are guilty of stating the obvious, here are some examples I've spotted in novels:

✗ Blinking her eyes
As opposed to blinking her elbows? Similarly, 'Nodded his head' and 'shrugged their shoulders'
✗ Holding the club gripped firmly in his hand
To 'grip' means 'hold firmly' and what part of a person's anatomy could be gripping a club other than their hand? All you need here is 'Gripping the club'.

Parroting regulations

Documents needed for regulatory compliance don't need to parrot the regulations themselves, especially as most regulations are appallingly written in the first place. For example, just because the Solvency II Directive (EU insurance legislation) says, 'Insurance and reinsurance undertakings shall have a regular cycle of model validation which includes monitoring the performance of the internal model, reviewing the ongoing appropriateness of its specification, and testing its results against experience' you don't have to parrot back:

✗ In order to ensure the ongoing appropriateness of our model's specification, we …
✓ We …

The same principle applies to other situations where you're responding to written requests for information, such as questionnaires.

Repeating words in tables and bullets

If you find yourself repeating the same words in every row of a table, put the text in the relevant column header instead. For example, instead of this:

Colour	*Means*
Red	*The data is* deleted
Amber	*The data is* modified
Green	*The data is* new

Table 1.4 Text duplicated per row

You can have this:

Colour	*Means* the data is …
Red	Removed
Amber	Modified
Green	New

Table 1.5 Duplicated text moved to header

Similarly, you can remove redundant columns by putting the text in the lead-in sentence instead. For example, suppose you have a table listing decisions the board needs to make and you have a column called 'Agreed?' in which the answer for every row in the table is 'Yes' – all you need is a lead-in sentence that says, 'The board has agreed all of the following actions' and you can then simply delete the now-redundant column.

This 'add repeated text before' technique also works with bulleted lists:

✗ The report incorporates:

- *a review of* mortality tables
- *a review of* economic projections
- *a review of* lapse data

✓ The report incorporates *reviews of*:

- mortality tables
- economic projections
- lapse data

Stock phrases

Stock phrases usually contain redundant words you can cut with no loss of meaning. Common examples include: in order to (*to*); may be subject to change (*may change*); in the first instance (*first*); of an urgent nature (*urgent*); and until such time that (*until*).

Legalese is notorious for stock phrases stuffed with redundancy. For example, you never need to write 'for the avoidance of doubt' because whatever statement follows this phrase will remove any doubt anyway. And 'including' doesn't need to be inflated to 'including among others / (but not limited to)' because 'including' already contains the notion of a non-exhaustive list. And if you're continuing to do something, it doesn't need to be 'on an ongoing basis'.

Good writers sometimes call filler phrases throat-clearers, because they are equivalent to someone coughing before speaking. In fact, some people are so infected by corporatese that it affects their speech as well as their writing, eg:

✗ 'It is my expectation that' instead of 'I expect'
✗ 'Have a conversation with' instead of 'talk to'

Spoken throat-clearers are unpleasant but at least they're partially understandable, because speakers are spinning words while gathering their thoughts and it's impossible to edit what you've just said – but there's no excuse for throat-clearers in writing.

Intensifiers and 'puff' words

'Intensifiers' are words that intensify another word, eg *very* and *really*. Strictly speaking, intensifiers are all adverbs (they qualify adjectives or other adverbs) but most corporate documentation is full of other types of word used to puff up the writer's self-importance: what I call 'puff words'.

For example, a pompous ex-colleague once emailed me to say I couldn't have a document yet because he was, 'in the process of making material content changes to' said document (nine words) instead of merely *editing* it (one word).

Here are some examples of common puff words you can cut. Notice how there is no loss of meaning once the puff words have gone:

- Section 5 ~~explicitly~~ covers risk quantification
- ~~Industry~~ standard
- User requirements are ~~actively~~ considered
- The legal entity has a review process ~~in place~~

- The ~~specific~~ document is Risk Calibration Methodology
- Other liabilities use the same ~~underlying~~ methodology
- This summary ~~is a high-level overview~~

Apart from being verbose, intensifiers and other puff words can harm or even invert your intended meaning. For example, 'She was mean to my friend' sounds adult but 'She was *very* mean to my friend' sounds childish. Or how about this example? 'Don't worry about lending money to John: he's *very* honest' – that 'very' turns something binary (honest v not honest) into something graduated, which introduces doubt about John's honesty.

Puff words are best deleted, but with [intensifier + weak adjective] combinations another option is to use a more precise adjective, eg *~~very big~~* / *huge*. In fact, a good rule of thumb to apply is this:

> Use adjectives and adverbs only to add precision, not emphasis.

Words saying the same thing

As well as intensifiers, another common vice that ruins much corporate writing is pairing words that say the same thing. One pairing I see depressingly often is 'review and challenge' – to review means 'to challenge', hence 'The board reviews *~~and challenges~~* the annual results.'

This pairing problem arises partly from the fact that English has roots in both Anglo-Saxon and Latin (and a lot more languages besides). You see these twin roots most often in legalese, which is full of what are called *legal doublets*. Just a few examples will suffice:

- aid and abet
- care and attention
- legal and valid
- ways and means
- will and testament

Just the one word from such pairings suffices – and make it the simpler one.

Clichés

We all know what the words cliché and stereotype mean, but did you know that originally they meant the same thing? *Cliché* was simply the French equivalent of the English word *stereotype*, meaning a metal plate that printers in the old days cast from a mould of hand-assembled type to save time and effort when printing new editions of existing books. It's why both words became pejorative terms for a fixed idea cast from someone else's words or actions.

The clichés we need to recast are not just the everyday ones such as *avoid like the plague* but also overused business words and our own stylistic tics. And before we go any further, be aware that cloaking a cliché with the word 'proverbial' doesn't hide it:

✗ No one dared to mention the *proverbial* elephant in the room.

Sorry, writer. We can all still see your elephant, and it's crapping on your credibility.

And still on the subject of linguistic crap, let's now turn to business clichés. And when I say 'business clichés' I'm sure you know exactly which words I'm referring to, the ones so overdone and dull that just seeing them makes your eyelids droop, words such as:

✗ solutions, challenges, leverage, synergy, articulate (as a verb), appropriately, reach out, passionate, embedded, offerings, around (eg 'based around' for 'based on')

Sometimes these clichés are ill-fitting as well as boring: a bullet might be 'embedded' (ie buried and immobile) in its target, so isn't it better to call an 'embedded' process 'operational'? A more serious problem is that these clichés are often ambiguous:

✗ practices that we could *leverage [introduce / adapt / develop / …?]*
✗ The calculation is *robust [reliable / transparent / efficient / …?]*

Opposite to clichés are words so fresh or even incongruous you can't help but remember them, like seeing someone wearing a pineapple as a hat. Now tell me without glancing back: which two words from the previous sentence stick most in your memory?

If you need inspiration, a thesaurus can help you find words that are both zestier and more accurate. Try www.thesaurus.com or www.onelook.com/thesaurus.

Also, make sure you avoid everyday clichés. Unless you can think of a truly fresh image, write your ideas plainly. Just as *She ran like the wind* is improved by being stripped back to *She ran*, so *It's a departmental hot potato* is improved if rewritten as *No one wants to touch this problem*. It's still a tactile image – but without the staleness.

Finally, watch out for personal clichés. Every writer has stylistic tics, such as pet words or phrases. I know I do. If you're aware of your foibles, it's worth doing a search-and-replace to check you haven't overused them. And if you're not aware of them, consider asking a reviewer to check for any over-repeated words and phrases – or consider investing in grammar-checking software that does the same thing.

SIMPLIFY YOUR SENTENCES

Now we've trimmed the fat and staleness, we can focus on making the sentences left over as clear as possible.

Replace light verbs with full verbs

A verb is full if its meaning is self-evident (eg *decide* or *bake*) and light if it needs other words to be understood (eg *make*, which needs expanding to 'make a decision' or 'make a cake'). Similarly, compare the full verbs *produce*, *act*, *present* and *review* with their light equivalents *enable* (the production of), *take* (action), *give* (a presentation), and *do* (a review of).

Replacing light verbs with full verbs confers several advantages. First (and as we've just seen), light verbs are verbose. For example, compare *facilitate the calculation of* with *calculate* and *is appropriate on an ongoing basis* with *remains appropriate*.

Second, light verbs obscure actions whereas full verbs highlight them:

✗ To *enable* the tracking of a document, it is also important that consistent naming conventions be *used*

✓ *Name* documents consistently so that they are easy to *track*

Third, light verbs are often ambiguous whereas full verbs aren't. For example, if you write that 'A *enables* B' you'll leave readers wondering whether A causes B or is merely a precondition for B:

✗ The interface *enables the saving of* data requests

✓ The interface *saves* data requests

Fourth, light verbs place a heavier cognitive load on readers than full verbs. For example, the word or phrase clarifying a light verb is often separated from the verb, forcing readers to retain a lot of information before they can complete their understanding:

✗ Market extremes could *make* the chosen risk factor distribution *invalid*

✓ Market extremes could *invalidate* the chosen risk factor distribution

Fifth, light verbs often hide missing information whereas full verbs expose it. For example, if you talk of 'making a decision' the idea sounds complete – what do we need to make? A decision! By using a full verb instead you expose the missing information, namely decide *what*?

✗ We need *to* make a decision
✓ We need to *decide* ___?

Sixth, changing the lightest verbs of all (*to be* and *to have*) into full verbs has the enormous benefit of changing descriptions (which are static) into actions (which are dynamic). For example, 'I eat' describes an action whereas 'I am' or 'I have' don't. So replacing *be/have* with other verbs energises your text:

✗ Megasoft *is* a software company *[lacks action]*
✓ Megasoft *creates* software for … *[more dynamic]*

On extremely rare occasions, 'to be' can function as a stronger verb than what's there already, eg the following sentence I once edited in a policy:

- The response will typically ~~*take the form of*~~ *be* a paper submitted to

That said, in all but the rarest cases you want to avoid the verbs *be/have* as much as possible. A hardcore form of English called E-Prime (short for English-Prime) even advocates avoiding the verb *to be* in all its forms to force you to clarify your thinking and strengthen your writing! That's extreme, but replacing *be/have* with fuller verbs wherever possible does undoubtedly improve your writing.

And finally, we've reached my favourite reason for replacing light verbs with full verbs: doing so kills nominalisations, namely nouns made from verbs. Nominalisations are those prose-choking words that typically end with *-tion*, *-ment* and *-ance*, words such as *calculation, requirement, compliance* – and, funnily enough, the word *nominalisation* itself. They're linguistic weeds, and they sprout wherever you have light verbs.

Why are nominalisations so hateful? Well, first off they turn actions (verbs) into states (nouns) so they are literally static and have to be nudged into action by a verb. Typically what happens is that the writer uses a light verb then realises it doesn't do the job ('make a what? a decision!') – but fails to replace the [light verb + noun] construction with the right verb for the job (*decide*). For example, why oh why write *develop a conceptual understanding* (as I once saw written in a policy I had to hack down to size) when you can use the perfectly serviceable verb *understand*? Or write *during the duration of the project* (yes, seriously, I saw this once) when you can write *during the project*?

Second, nominalisations suck the life from prose; no wonder the writing scholar Helen Sword calls them 'zombie nouns' and Steven Pinker calls them 'verbal coffins'. There's a lengthiness and heaviness to them that makes prose leaden and dull (calculation v calculate, production v produce), which probably explains why the noun *expenditure* is losing ground to *spend* (as a noun). But even when the noun's the same word as the verb, a verb's better: why write the ugly and clunky *increase spend* instead of the more natural *spend more*?

Third, nominalisations disguise cause and effect, which is why bureaucrats and spin-doctors love them:

✗ Firing from allied troops resulted in the killing of civilians
✓ Allied troops killed civilians
✗ The submission has been subject to an extensive governance process
✓ The submission has been extensively governed

Another reason that the sense of cause and effect is stronger in the shorter versions is that the important words are physically closer to each other. George Lakoff and Mark Johnson's previous mentioned *Metaphors We Live By* gives a subtle example:

- I found that the chair was comfortable
- I found the chair comfortable

The first sentence leaves open the possibility that I learnt of the chair's comfort indirectly (eg through a survey) whereas the second clearly refers to direct experience (ie sitting on the chair or touching it).

Nominalisations can be useful, as Joseph M Williams and Joseph Bizup observe in *Style: Lessons in Clarity and Grace*, eg:

✓ To refer to a previous sentence ('The board accepted this *decision*')
✓ To name the object of a verb ('We validated ~~*what was calculated*~~ > <u>*the calculation*</u>')

Notice, however, that these nominalisations are effective because they accompany strong verbs rather than light ones:

✗ The board *enabled the acceptance of* this decision
✓ The board *accepted* this decision

Minimise phrasal verbs

'Phrasal verbs' are verbs modified by an extra word (eg *up*, *out*, *down*, *off*, *on*) called a particle. Phrasal verbs are OK when the only alternative is a clunky Latinate verb, eg '*Put out* the fire' sounds more natural than '*Extinguish* the fire' – but under any other circumstances it's best to avoid them, and here's why.

First, phrasal verbs can be confusing, because they often sound similar to each other but have entirely different meanings. Imagine being a non-native speaker trying to understand sentences such as, 'The milk went off so I went off to the shops', 'She put him up but couldn't put up with him' or 'They got on with each other, so they got off with each other.' Similarly:

✗ *Write down* the meeting minutes so I can *write up* the proposal
✓ *Record* the meeting minutes so I can *write* the proposal
✗ *Set up* the risk categories, as *set out* in the documentation
✓ *Create* the risk categories, as *explained* in the documentation

Second, phrasal verbs are often verbose:

✗ Carry out a risk assessment > Assess risks
✗ Setting up network segmentation > Segmenting networks
✗ Push back on the date for > Reschedule

Third, phrasal verbs are easy to get wrong. People often miswrite them as one word or hyphenated, so avoiding them eliminates this risk:

✗ Setup [or *Set-up*] the database

You can see that the verb needs to be two words because the *-ing* form doesn't work as one word (you can't write *settingup*). Therefore:

✓ (*verb*) *Set up* the database
✓ (*noun*) *Setup* [or *Set-up*] *for* the database

If two nouns form a verb, however, you *do* hyphenate them or write them as one word:

✓ to spot-check, to backtest, to baseline

Again, the *-ing* test shows that these words are right, because (unlike 'settingup') you *can* write spot-checking, backtesting and baselining.

Fourth, phrasal verbs often sound like slang. Yes, I know I keep saying that a conversational tone is good, but phrasal verbs often sound just lazy and sloppy, the written equivalent of chewing gum while talking:

✗ *carry out, set up, get down to*
✓ *perform, organise, start*

Fifth, phrasal verbs are often light, meaning they're vague. To refresh your memory, verbs are light if they need other words to be understood, such as *make* (a decision? a cake?) and full if they don't (*decide*, *bake*) – in fact, it's this very lightness that explains why they're phrasal verbs in the first place, because they need an extra word (the particle) as a crutch. As a result, phrasal verbs provide a tempting copout from finding the best verb. Which is fine for lazy writers, but tough on their readers who are left puzzling over fuzziness such as:

- This project plan *sets out* [*proposes / clarifies / mandates / ...?*] the work required.

Finally, phrasal verbs are often tedious. The reason is that if you keep on using them it's hard to let go of them. (Whoops! Two phrasal verbs in that last sentence – you see how insidious they are?) And the more they occur, the more tedious they become. After bog-snorkelling through sludge such as ...

> The risk categories are *set up* in the risk log. The calibration methodologies are *set out* in the calibration document. The validation is *carried out* by the risk team, and the validation process is *set out* in the validation document.

... even the most determined reader starts to drown.

Simplify sentence structures

If readers, particularly when they are reading about complex topics, are forced to plough through complicated sentence structures – such as this one, which has lots of subordinate clauses (nested ideas, in other words) – they will quickly find (as you will as well) that your sentences are hard to follow, and (a significant secondary problem) give an impression of hesitancy and muddled thinking, because all those asides sound like qualifications (or hesitations, if you prefer) and afterthoughts.

Why is it so hard to understand complicated sentences, like the parody sentence above? Several reasons. First, remember the recency effect, namely the fact that we remember best what comes at the end? With long sentences, readers are likely to forget the start by the time they reach the end. And remember those limits to working memory (Miller's law of 7±2 items and more recent research suggesting it's only 3–5)? Long sentences can easily contain more than three ideas, relating to each other in complex ways. It's tough on readers – and on you as the writer, having to keep track of the syntax so your sentences don't derail.

Use simple structures. Subject-verb-object (SVO) is good. In fact, for business writing it's the best structure of all because virtually every type of company document falls into the pattern of 'actor does action', which equates grammatically to SVO:

- Processes: Who or what does what?
- Procedures: Who does what?
- Policies: Who has to do what?
- Guidelines: Who does what and how?
- Functional specs: What does what?
- Contracts: A must do X, B must do Y
- Requests for proposals: Who needs what?
- Sales and marketing material: Who wants to buy what, and why?

And just as SVO is good, so too is sticking to one idea per sentence. If you've written a sentence like the parody at the start of this section, unpack the ideas and deliver them in simpler sentences.

For example, try reading this sentence:

✗ When someone leaves the company, their access to all IT systems, including third party, SAP, Linux, mainframe, Active Directory, mobile devices, VPN tokens, and digital certificates, must be removed.

It's hard to read because there's a big lump of secondary information (all those examples of IT systems) you have to hold in your head before you get to the point of the sentence. The trick here is to move the secondary information into a second sentence:

✓ When someone leaves the company, their access to all IT systems must be removed. 'IT systems' includes third-party systems, SAP, Linux, mainframe, Active Directory, mobile devices, VPN tokens, and digital certificates.

Be aware that the problem here is not long sentences as such but ones that are needlessly convoluted. Varying sentence lengths injects life into your text, something we'll explore later.

Also note that sometimes a longer sentence is more elegant than two short ones, especially if it unifies an idea (such as cause leading to effect) and cuts words at the same time:

- The application was approved by the board~~. *It was*~~ then submitted to the regulator.

Let's look at some more reasons for reordering sentences.

First, to move a word further towards the front of a sentence so the reader's understanding isn't held in suspension. In the following example, look at all those adjectives (operational what? market what? credit what?) that don't make sense until the final word of the sentence:

✗ Mega Insurance Group produces methodology and calibration papers for operational, market, credit, and reinsurance credit default *risks*

✓ Mega Insurance Group produces methodology and calibration papers for *the following risks*: operational, market, credit, and reinsurance credit default

Second, to impose symmetry. In the following example, notice how the original sentence has a jarring shift from naming then describing a document to doing the reverse, whereas the rewrite imposes the same structure both times:

✗ The risk manual explains how risks are assessed. How risk affects product pricing is described in the actuarial manual

✓ The risk manual describes how risks are assessed, and the actuarial manual how they affect product pricing

Here's another example of imposing symmetry, this time changing a slightly distracting switch from adverb-verb to verb-adverb so they're both adverb-verb. You could, of course, have made them both verb-adverb instead, the point being that they're the same structure in each case:

✗ Ensure that policies and guidelines are correctly documented and reviewed regularly

✓ Ensure that guidelines and authorities are correctly documented and regularly reviewed

Third, to help readers understand what they have to do by putting verbs together. In the following example, notice how the original sentence forces you either to hold a lot information in your head or to reread the sentence once you get to the second action (Justify what? Ah, yes, excluded risk exposures):

✗ Identify any risk exposures excluded from the calculation *and justify why they are excluded*

✓ Identify *and justify* any risk exposures excluded from the calculation

Fourth, to put a modifying word closer to the word it modifies:

✗ Components are tested against non-functional requirements (eg scalability and performance tests) *regularly*
✓ Components are *regularly* tested against non-functional requirements, eg scalability and performance tests

Fifth, to replace a confusing structure of one idea nested inside another (what grammarians call 'centre embedding') with one idea followed by the next, which is much easier to understand:

✗ The risk appetite that the committee agreed was appropriate was approved
✓ The committee agreed and approved the risk appetite

Finally, to avoid starting a sentence with a description of an incomplete action ('Looking forward to next year') – a grammatical construction called a 'non-finite clause' that slams the brakes on the forward momentum of your text:

✗ Looking forward to next year, we see that the first quarter will be challenging
✓ The first quarter of next year will be challenging

Shift the weight in left-branching sentences

Earlier we explored how and why subject-verb-object (SVO) is such a powerful and clear way of giving people information. In this section, we'll examine two ways in which sentences often violate SVO – and how you can fix those that do.

The first common violation of SVO is one we looked at much earlier on – writing in the passive. Compare:

✓ Active: The dog bit the girl (SVO)
✗ Passive: The girl was bitten by the dog (OVS)

The second common violation is making readers' lives even harder by piling loads of information onto the 'O' (the recipient of the action), forcing readers to do a lot of cognitive 'heavy lifting' before they get to V (what's being done) and S (who's doing it).

Compare:

✗ The risk identification and assessment process must be documented by model owners
✓ Model owners must document how they identify and assess risks

Most people will find the second sentence clearer, and that's because:

- ✓ The sentence is active, not passive
- ✓ S and V come first, so we know straight away who (*model owners*) is doing what (*documenting*)
- ✓ We start with something simple (*model owners*) rather than complicated (*risk identification and assessment process*)
- ✓ It's easier to mentally process a big heavy phrase (that long 'noun string', aka stacked modifier) once you've got your head round the meaning of the sentence – a principle that Steven Pinker (in his book *The Sense of Style*) calls 'saving the heaviest for last'.

Whenever I encounter a 'heaviest first' sentence, I think of it as being like an unbalanced seesaw with the reader struggling to lift the heavy side. Your job is to lighten the reader's load by shifting the fulcrum (the verb, on which the sentence's action tilts) as far to the left as possible.

In English grammar, sentences with the subject and verb up front and the heavy bit at the end are known as 'right-branching' – and this 'lighter load' principle means they're nearly always preferable to left-branchers. That said, the *occasional* left-brancher inserted at opportune moments to inject variety into your prose is OK (this sentence being an example). As with so much in writing, it's about developing good judgement and a sense of balance. But do tip the balance in favour of right-branchers.

Let's see the steps to get from the difficult sentence to the easy one, bearing in mind that once you're familiar with the principles you'll be able to skip the intermediary steps:

1 Examine the structure of the original sentence:

The risk identification and assessment process *[left-branching abstract noun string]*
... must be documented *[passive]*
... by model owners *['doer' in the sentence comes last]*

2 Put the 'doer' first, to shift from active to passive:

Model owners *[doer comes first / subject is short and clear]*
... must document *[active]*
... the risk identification and assessment process *[still clunky]*

3 Unstitch the noun string:

Model owners *[short]*
... must document *[active]*
... how risks are identified and assessed *[clearer, but because it's passive it's unclear that the doer is 'model owners']*

4 Change the remaining passive construction to active:

Model owners *[short]*
... must document *[active]*
... how they identify and assess risks *[active – it's now clear that it's the model owners themselves who have to do this]*

Make sentences structurally parallel

Check for clumsy shifts in syntax:

✗ The committee recommends *accepting the proposal but that the price be renegotiated*
✓ The committee recommends *accepting the proposal but renegotiating the price*

The rewrite shows what grammarians call 'structural parallelism' or 'parallel structure', an old rhetorical trick for creating elegant and memorable prose.

REVISE FOR STYLE AND EMOTION

Now that your text is factually clear, you can concentrate on making it more emotionally engaging and simpler. Yes, *simpler*. Writing in an overblown style is usually a defence mechanism to make small ideas sound big, much in the way that a pufferfish inflates its body to many times its normal size to scare away predators – but it's bad psychology and counterproductive.

To convince yourself it's bad psychology, imagine you're deciding which of two business books to buy: the review for one says, 'Explains a complex topic in terms the layperson can understand – brilliantly clear and informative' while the other says, 'This writer must be really smart, because he used lots of big words and concepts I couldn't understand till I looked them up.' Which would you buy?

If this homely example doesn't convince you, consider that psychologist Daniel M Oppenheimer found that people writing in a convoluted and overblown style to appear intelligent are perceived as being *less* intelligent than those who write simply. Hyunjin Song and Norbert Schwarz from the University of Michigan found that when they asked students to choose the riskiest of various fictional food additives, the additives whose names were harder to pronounce were perceived as being more dangerous. And when Matthew McGlone and Jessica Tofighbakhsh from the University of Texas tested the effect of changing a single word in aphorisms so they no longer rhymed, eg changing 'Caution and measure will win you treasure' to 'Caution and measure will win you riches,' people found the unrhymed versions less believable.

In short, if you want to be understood, if you want to be perceived as intelligent, if you want to be *believed*, you're best off making your writing what psychologists call cognitively fluent – pleasant to read and easy to absorb. So let's look at how we can achieve cognitive fluency.

Create an agreeable tone

Consider the tone of your text: is it positive, friendly and empathetic? Or is it in any way pompous, patronising, boastful, monotonous, jobsworthy, inappropriate, or otherwise alienating?

To create an agreeable tone, first avoid corporatese. It's by far the most common tonal problem and it's a mode of writing that bears no resemblance to anything any normal person would ever *say*. Is it a desire to sound important? Some are guilty of that, yes. But often I think it's the pressure to conform: all your colleagues write that way so you feel obliged to follow suit (or perhaps you've never learnt that writing any other way is even an option). Just remind yourself that outside of the office no one in their right mind would think or communicate in corporatese, so there's no need to do it inside the office either. For instance, if someone stopped you on the street and asked 'Can you tell me how to get to the train station?' you'd probably *say* something like:

✓ 'Keep going this way for about a hundred yards. When you see the Red Lion pub, turn right and it's in front of you.'

What you'd never say, as a lot of corporate documentation's written, is:

✗ In order to facilitate the station-attainment process, it is necessary for the pedestrian to proceed in a northerly direction until the Red Lion pub observation process is complete, after which the pedestrian is required to initialise a right-turning process until station finding is complete.

Similarly, on a building site you'll read short and practical warnings such as:

✓ Hard hats must be worn at all times

This sentence is a perfect model of concision, because it covers *what* (wearing of hard hats), *where* (on site, because that's where the notice is) and *who* (everybody) – a rare example of where a passive without a specified doer works because the *who* is implicit: 'I'm the site manager and I don't care if you're a hod carrier, the chief architect, an investor, the Queen or the Pope – if you're on my site you'll bloody well wear a hard hat!'

Suppose instead this concise warning was written in typical corporatese, something such as this:

✗ To ensure compliance with the safety measures in UK Site Management Quality Standards (UKSMQS) section 15.a.ii subclause 15(a) November 2017 revision 3, footnote 5, it is necessary that all site personnel and visitors wear hard hats in all places and throughout the duration of their time on site

Reading this, site visitors would likely be bonked on the head by a half-tonne lintel before they reached the end of the sentence.

The fix here is to imagine you're *talking* to the person you're writing for. It'll help you to write in a friendly, human manner. It's like the advice to smile on the phone: your tone will immediately become more welcoming and natural. And you'll instinctively adapt your writer's voice to suit your audience: polite and professional for clients, more relaxed for colleagues, and so on.

Note that what I'm advocating here is to *imagine* talking to your reader, not writing exactly as you talk. Listen to people actually talking and you'll hear lots of hesitations, repetitions, backtracking, trains of thought abandoned when they've barely started, interruptions, useless filler. What you're aiming for is akin to dialogue in a well-written novel: something that feels like natural speech, but with all the wrinkles of actual speech ironed out.

As well as writing as if you're talking to someone, the hard-hat example teaches us to cut the obvious. Builders know why they're being asked to wear hard hats. Similarly, in a data-security policy: '~~*In order to ensure that data is secure, you need to ensure that you*~~ use a complex password.' Or consider an anti-bribery policy: which of the following two warnings do you think is most likely to hit home?

✗ Failure to comply with this policy may result in disciplinary proceedings leading to a charge of gross professional misconduct and instant dismissal, and potentially (subject to applicable laws in the business unit's country of jurisdiction) the possibility of criminal proceedings being brought against the employee

✓ If you accept or offer a bribe, you risk being sacked, fined or going to prison

The hard-hat example also reminds us of something we looked at earlier, namely avoiding confusing the means with the objective. The true purpose of wearing a hard hat is so you don't get hurt, any regulation being only the means to that end. Similarly, when writing any instruction (be it a policy, procedure, or anything else) stick to telling people what they need to do (or not do) without preceding it with all that 'In order to comply with …' nonsense. Simple's best. As simple as, 'Lock your bike when you leave it somewhere public.'

Writing as if you're talking to your readers has other benefits too. For instance, to convey complex material without sounding like a know-it-all you can use conversational phrases such as 'I know this is complex but bear with me' or 'These results surprised me as well.' Similarly, you can deliver common knowledge without sounding patronising, by using phrases such as 'You probably know that …' (without appending *but*, which risks contradicting the *probably*). You can even subtly instruct readers on *how* to read your text, for example suggest they slow down when you've just hit them with something important or complex ('Let's stop to think about this for a moment').

You can also use a conversational approach to help readers feel they're equal partners with you in a voyage of discovery, rather than in a teacher/pupil power imbalance. TV documentary presenters do this all the time, with phrases such as 'In this episode we'll discover …' The script and filming have been planned or completed well in advance, so there's no 'discovery' for the presenter – but the artifice certainly helps us as viewers to feel we're equal partners in the midst of the action.

My final tip about creating a conversational tone is to use contractions (things such as *isn't, doesn't* and *won't* rather than *is not, does not* and *will not*). Despite what you may have been taught in school about contractions being 'wrong' in formal writing, they're not only OK but also often better than their stuffier counterparts. For example, imagine getting an email with one of these two sentences:

- You aren't allowed to do that
- You are not allowed to do that

Doesn't the second sentence sound a teeny bit angry?

Novelists use contractions all the time, and it's pretty well mandatory in dialogue if characters are to sound natural. That said, it's best not to go overboard: earlier I wrote *may have* rather than *may've*, which felt to me a touch too informal for the context (although I might well use it in dialogue). A second caveat about contractions is that readers with low literacy find them harder to read than full words. Again: know your readers.

A second way to create an agreeable tone is to address your readers directly as 'you' rather than writing as if they're absent (eg 'users must'). Think about conversations: they're always between me and you (first and second person) – the third person is the one who's excluded:

> Do you (*second person*) want to come to the pub with me (*first person*)?
> I don't know where they (*third person – absent*) have got to.

As with avoiding corporatese, the trick is to imagine you're talking to the person you're writing for. That way you'll naturally always stick to 'me and you':

✗ Megasoft's recommendations for the client are …
✓ We recommend that you …
✗ Reporting entities are required to …
✓ You must …

Third, replace pompous words (often Latinate) with simpler choices (often Anglo-Saxon). For example, compare the sour legalese tang of *upon request* with the clean taste of *when asked*. Or the deadening thump of *commence*, *demonstrate*, *facilitate*, *remediate*, *remunerate*, *articulate* and *utilise* with the lightness and freshness of *start*, *show*, *help*, *fix*, *pay*, *say* and *use* – the last of which has the further advantage of avoiding the UK/US conflict between *utilise/utilize*.

Ostentatious words can make you sound not only pompous but also ridiculous. I remember walking past a local newsagents whose sign announced reductions not on bags of sweets but on 'confectionary pouches' – the phrase sounded so like something the British comic character Alan Partridge would say, or some bizarre sexual innuendo, that I collapsed into a fit of giggles lasting for the rest of my walk to the train station.

Latinate words become even claggier when they expand to phrases, such as *per annum* instead of *each year*; or the unforgivable *inter alia*, which I spotted in particularly pompous document I once had to edit.

Fourth, avoid sounding unpleasant. Mercifully, this tonal problem's less common than the others but you must always be on your guard against using language that could be construed as condescending, insincere, grudging, sarcastic, blunt, or otherwise negative. Avoid talking down at people with phrases such as *simply*, *easily*, *obviously*, and *everyone knows*. Never send an email in anger. And if you're writing an apology, make sure it's gracious:

✗ A recent customer survey gave us a 90% satisfaction score, so we are surprised that you feel that our product was unsatisfactory. The product is within warranty, however, so please complete the attached form so we can process your refund.

✓ We're sorry you're unsatisfied with our product, and have given you a full refund.

Another tip for apologising is that it's good psychology to finish on a positive rather than negative note:

✗ Once again, we're sorry that …
✓ We look forward to …

If you're the one doing the complaining rather than responding to it, it's tempting to go in all guns blazing, fired up with righteous indignation. Don't. All you'll do is annoy (or amuse) the person with the power to help you. Think of teachers who lose their rag at the slightest provocation and how kids wind them up mercilessly just to see them explode. Another drawback of starting with all guns blazing is that if you later need to escalate the problem you've nowhere further to go – you just sound like the feeble old fool King Lear shaking his fist and ranting, 'I will do such things / What they are, yet I know not.'

If you're delivering bad news, you can avoid the twin perils of bluntness or squirming euphemism by delivering your message in the form positive-unpalatable-positive (a form that's crudely but memorably called a 'shit sandwich'):

✓ Thank you for submitting and presenting such a strong bid. After much debate we've chosen another supplier. But we were impressed by your products and you remain on our shortlist for future bids.

If you're delivering *really* unpalatable news, you may need to dispense with the top slice of bread to avoid creating an impression of insincerity or hypocrisy, and a justifiably angry reaction from the recipient. Compare, for example:

✗ Thank you for your service to our company – we appreciate all you've done for us over the past ten years. Unfortunately, the recession means that our profits are down and we have to let you go. *[If you think I'm such a great employee, why the hell are you firing me?!]*
✓ I'm sorry to have to bring you bad news. Despite our best efforts to keep every member of staff, large losses mean we're having to shut down your branch and hence having to let you go.

Always keep the bottom slice of the sandwich, though. For instance, in an email telling people they're losing their jobs, finish by thanking them for their service, and by telling them what redundancy package they can expect and any other measures you're taking to help them.

Finally, avoid writing sloppily or in textspeak. Doing so might be acceptable in rushed text messages between friends or family. But in any formal business context it reeks of arrogance because the subtext to your readers is, 'I'm too busy to bother writing properly to you. Heck, I'm so important and you're so beneath me you don't deserve the extra second it would take me to sign off my email with *Regards* instead of *rgds*.'

Even if you're the boss (*especially* if you're the boss – you should be setting an example!), even if you're thumbing an email into your mobile while straphanging on the train to work, don't write sloppily. Readers don't know where and how you typed your message: all they see is something written without care. And when that's the case, why should they be bothered to *read* with care?

Remove anything potentially offensive

Most writers are naturally careful about avoiding sexist language ('the actuary … *he*') and the best avoidance technique is to use plurals ('actuaries … *they*'), which avoids clumsy constructions such as 'the actuary … *(s)he*'. Easier to miss are words written in innocence that could cause offence. For example, if there's any risk that *blacklist / whitelist* could be construed as having a racist undertone, use *deny list / allow list* instead; similarly, '*disable* the feature' is potentially offensive whereas '*switch off* the feature' is not. Or how about this clanger from a business proposal I was given to edit?

✗ By merging concept and approach, the *final solution* …

Combined, these two words are so poisoned by the horrors of the Holocaust that they should never appear together in a business document:

✓ By merging concept and approach, the *complete solution* …

Here's another genuine example, an email I received from the head of security of an office block in the City of London, shortly after a terrorist attack left several people dead:

✗ We have increased the number of guards in the building, and *the additional bodies* will remain until further notice

✓ We have increased the number of guards in the building, and *they* will remain until further notice

Avoid egocentrism

Imagine your washing machine has flooded your kitchen. You phone one plumber who says, 'We'll be with you in 15 minutes and fix it within the hour.' You phone another who says, 'Mega Plumbing is dedicated to providing outstanding customer service. We have four divisions: Customer Care, Emergencies, Retail Sales, and Trade Sales.' Which plumber will you hire?

Or imagine you're climbing Everest in a snowstorm, the ice cracks under your crampons and your freezing hands slip through the rope, leaving you dangling two hundred feet over a ravine. Do you shout 'Help!' or 'Can someone sell me mountain-climbing consultancy, please?'

The lesson from both these examples is this: people are reading your document or marketing material because they care about their own problems, not yours. They want to buy your ideas, not be sold them.

How do you spot egocentric writing? And how do you fix it? Let's find out right now.

First, avoid overusing *I* or *me*, especially when your message ignores the reader's perspective. Here's a genuine example, an email I received from a recruitment agent:

> *I* hope you are well. *I'm* reaching out as *I'm* hoping that you might be able to assist *me* with a role *I* am working on. Currently *I'm* working with a Lloyd's insurer and *I'm* looking at two roles

Doesn't it just make your index finger itch to hit Delete? Suppose she'd written this instead:

> Given your experience, you're perfect for a brand-new role at a top Lloyd's insurer. Interested?

And how many websites have you read where the pages are called 'About Us', 'Our Values' and 'What We Do'? Where am I, your visitor, in all of this? Why should I care about 'your values' if I have to hunt around through endless pages of self-congratulation to find out whether you can help me?

The solution is to restructure your material according to the *needs > benefits > features* pattern we looked at earlier. But be warned that the needs that come first must be the reader's not yours. Take this sign I saw outside a convenience store:

> BEERS: 4 for 6

You can guess what the writer was thinking: 'I get paid for four (my need first) and I give you six (your need last).' Unfortunately for the seller, the buyer will inevitably misread the message by putting *their* needs first:

> BEERS: [I get] 4 for [the price of] 6

Not such a good deal!

Even when first person is the right viewpoint to adopt, make sure you don't have too many sentences (especially consecutive ones) starting with 'I'. A classic example is your CV, where you can often delete 'I' by changing sentences to a list – which not only eliminates the egocentrism but also highlights the verbs (ie what you achieved):

✗ *I* led a finance department of 15 staff. *I* managed a budget of £20 million and *I* reduced expenditure by 20%
✓ Achievements: *led* a finance department of 15 staff; *managed* a budget of £20 million; *reduced* expenditure by 20%

Another option for avoiding repeating 'I' at the start of too many sentences is to reshuffle your word order so that 'I' appears in the middle of sentences, where it's less obtrusive.

Second, avoid needlessly naming your company, department, and so on. Even text that's not overtly me-focused can contain unnecessary 'me' language, so look for any instances of naming your company, department, etc, that aren't strictly necessary. Suppose, for example, you're in the finance department and writing a report to help the board set next year's budget:

✗ Finance has consolidated all of last year's results to produce the projection for this year.

The board cares only about the results, not how Finance produced them:

✓ Below is this year's projection, based on last year's results.

Third, replace *I* with *you*. Any business text that's implicitly a conversation will have *I/we* for the company's viewpoint and *you* for the reader's viewpoint. For example, an insurance contract might say, 'We cover you for the first £200 but you must pay any excess.' In such cases, *I/we* is perfectly acceptable. But if there's no implicit conversation, *you* is always better. In the following example, notice how the first sentence makes you feel spoken *at* while the second makes you feel spoken *to*:

✗ I will supply a presentation pack next week
✓ You will receive your presentation pack next week

One caveat – avoid *you* if it sounds needlessly accusatory (and if criticism is needed, supporting facts count for more than an accusation):

✗ *Your* decision to cut costs puts the project at risk
✓ Cutting costs puts the project at risk, *because* …

Fourth, do your research and make it personal. Avoid generic mailshots that show you haven't bothered to research your recipients. A classic example is emails from recruitment agents that begin with, 'Apologies if this email has reached you in error,' compound the insult by describing a totally unsuitable job, and finish with a request that you do their job for them ('If you know anyone suitable …').

A bad recruitment agency pitch at least bears a modicum of relevance to the recipient. Even worse are cold pitches sent to completely the wrong people. I once received a LinkedIn message from a start-up mobile bank saying 'we now need $2.6 million at a new round for 20%' and asking 'Can we have a call & send a deck please?' A blunderbuss approach such as this, one that can't even differentiate between a business writer and angel investors, will just blow up in the sender's face and miss its target every time.

OK, these sorts of blunders can happen by accident if you're using a keyword-driven automated marketing tool. But if you do use such tools, for goodness' sake be a bit more careful before you pull the trigger. Better still, ditch the tools altogether and make the effort to handcraft invitations to a carefully selected audience. One hit is better than 10,000 misses. And does a hell of a lot less damage.

Fifth, change verbs to the reader's viewpoint. For example, if a company tells you to 'buy' their product, will you be inclined to do so? Here you can learn a trick from advertisers – instead of telling you to 'buy' something (seller's perspective) they invite you to 'discover' it (consumer's perspective).

We saw earlier that's usually best to change 'I' to 'you' so your reader feels spoken *to* rather than spoken *at*. A further advantage of switching from me to you is that it naturally forces a verb change, for example 'I will *supply*' to 'You will *receive*'. But be aware that while you-oriented writing is generally a good thing, it's important to keep a sense of balance: if you overdo it you risk sounding fawning or sarcastic, like those salespeople who've been told that customers like hearing their own names. We do. Just not every other bloody word.

My final tip for reducing egocentrism is to replace boasts with facts. Common red-flag phrases include *well established*, *widely regarded*, *track record*, *proven expertise*, *recognised as*, and *unparalleled* – all phrases that leave your reader thinking, 'Says who?' Unless you or your firm have won an award or have other evidence proving you really are the best, claiming so comes across as arrogant and delusional. Just as speaking quietly is often a more effective way to get people to listen than shouting, quieter words are often the ones that speak loudest. Modesty encourages trust. And if your firm does have something to boast about, facts are far more eloquent than opinion:

✗ Across multiple industry sectors, Megasoft creates the most powerful and feature-rich business software.
✓ Megasoft's GoldProspect is used by tier-1 banks and insurers, including <list of clients>, and has won <award name> every year since 2015.

Even if you can't find one single quantifiable fact (really?), or the facts are lukewarm, at least try to get a customer testimonial: praise from anyone else is far more believable than self-praise.

To get the full impact of why boastful text is a turn-off, imagine a person saying it rather than a company: 'Across multiple industry sectors, I create the most powerful and feature-rich business software.' Sounds conceited or delusional, right? Speaking of which, take a look right now at your CV and LinkedIn profile: if you spot anything with a whiff of self-congratulation or cliché such as 'talented, results-driven professional with extensive experience' or 'passionate' (a word that's slumped to junk-bond status) replace it with facts about what you've done and let readers infer how great you are. It's *way* more convincing:

✗ Outstanding salesperson, passionately driven to increase the sales of every company I work for
✓ Led a team of 15 salespeople, and increased our department's profits by 32% within one year

The second one feels so much more credible than the boasting, doesn't it? One reason is that value judgements are vague; facts are not. Take a statement such as, 'He received a huge pay rise' – a CEO will have a very different figure in mind compared to a cleaner, whereas 'He received a pay rise of £150,000 plus stock options worth an additional £100,000' leaves no room for doubt. Copywriters call such quantifiable facts 'proof points' – and a marketing message lacking any proof '… is a tale / Told by an idiot, full of sound and fury / Signifying nothing'.

Make abstractions concrete

One reason our minds glaze over when we read phrases such as 'To facilitate the operation of the data-management process' is that all the nouns are abstract rather than concrete, namely recognisable through the senses.

The words fail to paint a picture or otherwise touch our senses. Compare:

✗ It was cold, windy and wet
✓ The girl shivered under a flapping umbrella

Novelists call this technique 'showing, not telling'. Even the driest 'tell' explanation can often be enlivened with a 'show' example, anecdote, or vivid simile or metaphor. Oh, before we go further, if you're unsure of (or can't remember) the difference between similes and metaphors, here's a mnemonic to help you:

> Similes are *similar* ('O my Luve is *like* a red, red rose'), whereas metaphors *metamorphose* because one thing becomes another ('a sea of troubles').

So, similes and metaphors – fine for the likes of Rabbie Burns and Shakespeare, but can you really use them in business documents? Yes, and they can make your ideas vivid and memorable, and (as long as you don't mix your metaphors) provide thematic continuity across an extended line of thought:

✗ House prices *dived* in March despite *healthy* overseas investment, before *climbing* again in September
✓ House prices *crashed* in March despite *solid* overseas investment, before *building* again in September

Another trick with metaphors is to use ones that appeal to multiple senses: not just sight but also sound, touch, and taste/smell. Think how often we use multisensory metaphors in everyday speech: 'I *see* what you're saying, and the idea *rings a bell*. Let's *grab* a coffee and talk about it.'

Avoid seemingly concrete imagery that's so vague it distracts your readers. Take this lazy sentence I read in a crime novel. The scene was the hero visiting a former slaughterhouse where a young girl had been found murdered, something that should have been packed with tension and vividness:

✗ There are birds hanging about.

I found myself so caught up with trying to picture what the writer meant (What kinds of birds? And what's a bird doing when it's 'hanging about'? Am I supposed to visualise starlings screeching and wheeling? Crows pecking at bloodstained rags? Something else?) that this wretched sentence snapped me out of the fictional dream.

Also, make sure you avoid metaphors likely to repel your readers. I once encountered 'deepening wallet share', which the writer presumably meant as a euphemism for 'getting clients to spend more money'. It certainly creates a concrete image: but, alas for the writer, it's that of a nimble-fingered pickpocket eyeing you up as a mark.

Finally, take advantage of the fact that metaphors work with pictures as well as words. Infographics are great at this. Returning again to that snoozefest presentation we simplified verbally, you could *visually* represent a profit loss in aviation using something such as this:

Figure 1.5 Infographic for simplifying numerical data

Infographics such as this are far more impactful and memorable than the usual bar charts and pie charts. And to get inspiration for infographics you need look no further than your computer's user interface, with its intuitive icons of folders, envelopes, trashcans, and suchlike.

Consider connotations

Two words can *denote* (ie describe) the same thing but *connote* (ie suggest) different things, so always heed connotations. Take 'moist' and 'damp' – both mean 'between wet and dry' but would you rather eat a moist cake or a damp cake? Buy a new home, or be sold a residential unit? Similarly, would you rather be called a 'person' (a human being) or a 'resource' (something exploited and discarded)? And as for 'candidate pipeline', a vile term I once heard uttered by a head of HR, what gets flushed down a pipeline? Yes, exactly.

Think of a word's connotations as being its emotional charge: as the psychologist and linguist Steven Pinker has explained, while denotations are stored in the neocortex (the most recent part of the human brain, responsible for higher cognitive functions such as reasoning and planning), connotations are stored in the limbic system (a primitive part of the brain responsible for our emotional life, including fear, reward and the mating instinct). No wonder connotations make words more striking and memorable!

A dramatic example of how connotations affect perception is a psychological experiment conducted by psychologists Elizabeth Loftus and John Palmer at the University of Washington in 1974. When people were shown short film clips of a car crash, their estimates of the cars' speeds could be manipulated simply by changing the verb used to ask the question: those told the cars *contacted* each other estimated 31.8 mph but those told the cars *smashed into* each other estimated 40.8 mph – a remarkable 22% difference.

Emotionally charged language gives a similar uplift to readership figures. Just listen to any politician, or look at tabloid headlines: killers aren't 'imprisoned' but 'caged', jilted lovers aren't 'unhappy' but 'furious', 'surprising' becomes 'shocking', and so on. I'm not suggesting you write like a tabloid journalist (unless you *are* one) – but you do need to consider emotional impact and hence choose your words wisely.

Finally, be aware that even abstract words that look similar can have different connotations, eg:

- *simple / simplistic* (negative because it means 'over-simplified')
- *complex* (the human brain is 'complex' and that's a good thing) / *complicated* (negative because it means 'unnecessarily complex')
- *assertive / aggressive* (never 'aggressive sales and marketing', unless you're running an extortion racket)

Arouse curiosity

One of the best ways to engage your readers is to promise them something – just as I promised earlier that I'd show you 'How to write any document'. Did you feel drawn in by that promise? And have the questions throughout this guide drawn you in as well, making you feel as if you're being talked *to* rather than talked *at*? Promises and questions are great for arousing curiosity, as you'll notice from all adverts, magazines and self-help books that use them:

> Get a beach-ready body in only a month!
> Discover the 7 secrets of successful people
> What does your favourite colour reveal about you?

If your heading poses a question, make sure it's one that compels your reader to read on:

✗ Is your IT system secure? *[If your reader thinks 'of course it is!' you've lost them]*

✓ How secure is your IT system? *[Reader worries – and reads on]*

The above example works by turning a closed (yes/no) question into an open question. But even a closed question can be phrased to make your reader itchy for answers. Compare these two questions, both of them closed:

✗ Happy with your home insurance? *[Yes/no – so little incentive to read on]*
✓ Paying too much for your home insurance? *[Am I? Better read on …]*

But whatever question you raise, make sure your body text answers it. Think of the golden rule of barristers in court, namely to ask only questions to which you already know the answer. Think of all those crime dramas where the barrister says something such as, 'But you lied about where you were on the night of the murder, didn't you? It's written here, in the police report.'

Incidentally, turning a statement into a question is a great way to increase the likelihood that people will respond to your emails, because social norms condition us to answer direct questions. Compare:

✗ Please confirm whether you're still coming to Tuesday's 3 pm meeting
✓ Are you still coming to Tuesday's 3 pm meeting?

As well as promises and questions, what are also effective are the kinds of cliffhanger phrases people use when telling a good story, the ones that make you want to lean in to hear more: phrases such as, 'But that's not all.' Yes, the golden rule 'Know your audience' applies and in more sober contexts such as board reports you may want to stay the right side of chatty. On the other hand, you may be surprised at how even those people you fear are stuffed shirts breathe with relief when your prose undoes its top button.

Excite your readers

We've just explored how word connotations can affect our emotional responses. More profoundly, to persuade your readers to act you *must* engage their emotions. The neuroscientist Antonio Damasio made a fascinating discovery: people with brain impairments that prevent them from feeling emotions are unable to make decisions. They can describe choices logically but are mentally paralysed when forced to make even the simplest choices, such as what to eat.

Another neuroscientist, Dr Adrian Owen, in his fascinating book *Into the Grey Zone*, gives an even more extreme example of the essential role of emotion in engaging the brain. His challenge was finding a way to stimulate the brain activity of people in a persistent vegetative state such that their emotions could be reliably interpreted. After some trial and error, guess what he and his team discovered? 'The brain loves movies by Alfred Hitchcock. That's probably because they are constructed to make us think, fear, anticipate, expect, and react.'

Or think of advertising: a TV advert for cars doesn't reel off a list of data but instead shows a sexy, smiling person speeding through a movie-style setting such as romantic Parisian streets or twisting Alpine roads. Or take a bar of chocolate: advertisers never sell you the facts; on the contrary, the ingredients are hidden on the back of the packaging in small lettering. Instead, they usually awaken your senses with a message such as 'Discover the pleasure of melting into a creamy mouthful of delight.' (Is it really chocolate they're selling?)

It works the other way too, in that reasons endorse emotions. As the famous adman David Ogilvy once said, 'Customers need a rational excuse to justify their emotional decisions. So always include one.' Going back to chocolate, imagine an advert that has a photo of cupcakes and how much more powerful the copy would be if instead of saying merely 'Indulge yourself' it said 'Indulge yourself (only 150 calories so you can).'

Play on fears

We've just seen how exciting your readers is an effective way to persuade them – what can be even more powerful is playing on their fears. Sounds a bit nasty, doesn't it? I'm not talking here about threats ('Buy this or we shoot the puppy' or 'We know where your kids go to school') but good old loss aversion. Which one of us hasn't been persuaded to do something out of a fear of missing out (FOMO)?

Old advertising lines such as 'But hurry – stocks are limited!' might sound cheesy but they work. So if you want people to act, suggest a scarcity of resources ('places are limited!'), scarcity of time ('offer ends tomorrow!') or play on FOMO ('Over 500 of your fellow professionals have already signed up').

Be humorous

One incredibly effective way to engage readers, hardly ever used in corporate documentation, is humour. If you're looking for inspiration, pick up any newspaper or magazine and you'll soon find headings using humour (especially puns) – even in publications you might expect to be humourless. Take this risqué heading I once spotted in the *Financial Times*:

> Viagra faces stiff competition

Humour doesn't, of course, have to be vulgar (and in many cases vulgarity may be extremely ill advised) – and even the most innocent humour can fall flat. That said, that Viagra headline does illustrate just how vivid and memorable well-targeted humour can be. Even a gentle pun or subtle cultural reference can spice up a dry article, and puns often pack a lot of meaning into a few words while also piquing our curiosity. For example, here are three boring article headings rewritten to inject humour:

✗ Challenges facing insurers
✓ Risky business
✗ Factors affecting contract renewals
✓ Contract killers
✗ Underwriting errors to avoid
✓ Blunderwriting

Surprise your readers

What colour is a shadow? If you said 'grey or black', look at how a good painter represents shadows and you'll see that they can be lilac, green, blue and many other colours, depending on the surrounding objects and light conditions.

Good writers know that words too are coloured and nuanced by their context; that what creates the biggest emotional impact is not fancy words disguising clichéd thinking but simple words in startling combinations. Take the line 'As two tall ships, wind-mastered, wet with light' from Philip Larkin's poem *Love we must part now*. Could there be three simpler words than 'wet with light'? But oh, what an explosion of sensations they create when combined: you can see those sails glistening with water and sun (or moonlight); and how achingly sad and beautiful those three words become when resonating with the imagery in the rest of the poem.

Or take John Updike's beautiful description, in his novel *Couples*, of a woman pinching her earring 'as if it had chimed' – I bet you can *see* that earring even though it's been described in terms of *sound*. Or Margaret Atwood's brilliant use of an adjective in her novel *The Blind Assassin* (which won the Man Booker Prize) where she describes sad-looking shrubs as 'disgruntled' – an example of personification, namely attributing human characteristics to something nonhuman, which is a great way to inject life into your prose (and note too the sound echo in 'disgruntled shrubs' – no surprise that Atwood was a poet before becoming a novelist).

How can you add a little poetry to your own writing? One very simple technique is simply to pause whenever you're tempted to write the first word that comes to mind and search your imagination for a different word, a *surprising* word. Suppose, for example, you're given the challenge of completing the simile 'shining like <something>'. Most of us would reach for the most obvious word: 'shining like the *sun*', perhaps. Or given the phrase '<something> like honey' we'd probably go for sticky or sweet. Isn't it so much more interesting and memorable to combine these two ideas to create something new, to write 'shining like honey' as the poet Mary Oliver did in her poem *Whispers*?

I call such poetic combinations '*un*-predictive text' – so every time you find yourself grabbing the first word that comes to mind, the one your mobile phone's predictive text would suggest, pause a moment and find a word that's fresh. With this technique alone, you'll elevate your writing above that of 99% of your colleagues.

Most true writers have favourite writerly phrases they can quote by heart, and one of the best ways to improve your writing is to find your own favourites and think about why they touch you. Just as you are what you eat, so too you are what you read.

Going back to context for a moment, read the following list of words and try to remember them as best you can (example taken from *The Self Illusion*, by Bruce Hood):

thread, pin, eye, sewing, sharp, point, prick, thimble, haystack, thorn, hurt, injection, syringe, cloth, knitting

Put your hand over the list so you can't see it – which of these words is in the list?

needle, river

Look at the list again. See how powerful context can be?

Listen to your writing

Before writing came speech, and our ears can often detect what our eyes miss. So let's look at (or rather *listen to*) the many ways in which hearing your text can help you to improve and correct it. We'll start by getting a feel for the difference between editing with your eyes and with your ears. Here's a paragraph deliberately written to be monotonous. First, *look* at the following paragraph to *see* what makes it so:

> Here is some ordinary text. It is written in a clear style. It has no grammatical errors. It says what it needs to and nothing more. It should be OK. This does not feel quite right. There are faults but you cannot find them.

What you probably *saw* is that four consecutive sentences start with *It* and the others start with equally meaning-starved words such as *There*, and *This* stripped of its referent (namely the thing that 'this' is referring to):

> *Here* is some ordinary text. *It* is written in a clear style. *It* has no grammatical errors. *It* says what it needs to and nothing more. *It* should be OK. *This* does not feel quite right. *There* are faults but you cannot find them.

Now go back and say the paragraph out loud (or at least 'hear' it playing in your mind's ear).

Did you notice that it sounded stilted? Monotonous? Perhaps you found your inner voice sounding like a robot. The problem with the paragraph, easier to hear than to see, is rhythmic – every sentence is roughly the same length so the paragraph lacks bounce and energy. It plods. The trick here is to listen to your text. If it *sounds* boring, vary your sentence lengths and rhythms to put a spring in your text. Note too that varying sentence lengths injects not only energy but also emphasis, because a short sentence after a long one really stands out. Look at this one.

Just as a lack of rhythm can harm your text, so too can clumsy rhythms: and again it's your ears that alert you, not your eyes. Try it now, by saying the following sentence out loud (or silently listening to it in your head):

✗ This chapter explains System X, in particular the installation and configuration

Did you feel yourself stumbling over the words, like over untied shoelaces? If so, remember the advice of Peggy Noonan, speechwriter for Ronald Reagan: 'Where you falter, alter.' Let's alter the rhythm right now:

✓ This chapter explains System X, especially how to install and configure it

You probably felt 'how to install and configure it' tripping off your tongue. But did you also notice how the tempo change of 'especially' emphasises the following word 'how', like the hop and skip in a triple jump?

As well as giving bounce and emphasis to a sentence, good rhythms can subtly echo meaning. For example, say out loud the following two sentences – can you feel the rat-tat-tat rhythm of the first and the de-duh heartbeat rhythm of the second, and how well those rhythms fit the meanings of their respective sentences?

✓ Somebody knocked on the door

✓ The blood was pumping in his veins

We've just explored the importance of listening for rhythmic problems with your text: another thing to listen for is how much vowel-sound variety you have, because it's vowels that animate speech and hence writing – a point made very eloquently by Joe Moran in his delightful book, *First You Write a Sentence*.

To feel the effect of vowel variety for yourself, concentrate on how it feels to say 'bish, bash, bosh' – or ping-pong, ding-dong, click-clack. The vowels feel alive, because your tongue is moving from the back of your mouth to the front to produce them. Such phrases in English invariably follow the vowel order I-A-O – and 'consistent order of tongue movement' is one theory for why it's so. Irrespective of whether the theory's true, what's undeniable is that vowel variety makes sentences come alive. For example, why do photographers ask us to 'say cheese'? Because that long *ee* forces us to stretch our lips into a smile.

Now say a word such as *conversation* and hear how it comes out sounding like *convuhsayshun*, with two of the vowel sounds an inert 'uh' that sits in the middle of your mouth, a sound known as *schwa*. And what sort of word is *conversation*? It's one of those dreaded nominalisations we explored earlier on, those nouns made from verbs (*reaction* from react, *movement* from move, and so on) that I said suck the life from prose. Here, then, is another reason that nominalisations kill prose: they *sound* dead. Consider all those *-ment*, *-tion* and *-ance* nominalisations: they're riddled with schwas. Try it now, by saying 'The development of the compliance regulation' – can you feel how the words lie dead in your mouth like a lump of lead?

In summary, whenever words feel lifeless in your mouth, be they nominalisations or anything else, replace them with words that vary the vowel sounds.

Another weakness your ears will spot better than your eyes is words whose sounds don't fit. What do I mean by this? Well, the mere sound of a word can give it an emotional colouration. If you attune your ears to these emotional nuances, you can often elevate your writing by changing a not-wrong word into the perfect word.

For example, if you're entering a room and want to be quiet, are you more likely to *shut* or *close* the door? If you're attuned to sound and tone, you probably instinctively said *close* – perhaps without even knowing why. I'd choose *close* as well and that's because of that long *oh* vowel and soft sibilance at the end – the sound itself closes slowly. In contrast, *shut* is short and percussive. It snaps shut. It sounds louder.

Another example. Imagine a scene in a novel where someone's doing the washing-up and you have to guess their emotions based on one of these two descriptions:

- Cutlery crashed against crockery
- Plates slid into the soapy water

Chances are you inferred anger from the first, and sadness or sensuality from the second. Why? There is *nothing* in those descriptions about emotions – but you *felt* the emotions from the contrast between harsh and soft sounds.

Listening to your text can also help you spot the following problems:

- Typos caused by similar-looking words: Take *thorough/through/though* or *enquires/enquiries* or *manger/manager*, and even *Polish/polish* – it's hard to see the differences, but easy to hear them.
- Awkward sound repetitions: Take a sentence such as, 'How and where we're transforming banking' and when you say it you'll stumble over that awkward *where were* – flip the word order and you produce the much smoother sounding sentence, 'Where and how we're transforming banking.'
- Comic or rude accidents: For example, say 'I eat beans and far too often' and you'll get wind of something amiss.
- Wrong punctuation: Noticing where you pause or breathe can help you spot wrong punctuation, particularly misplaced or missing commas.
- Convoluted sentences: If you run out of breath when saying a sentence, or find your natural pauses jerky or excessive, the sentence is probably convoluted.

FIX YOUR PUNCTUATION

Now we've got all of our sentences written as well as we can, we're going to zoom in even further and tweeze out any errors of punctuation, grammar and spelling. You'll typically check all three at the same time (it's no coincidence that Microsoft has a 'spelling and grammar' feature that does just that). But because punctuation is a vast topic in its own right, we're going to look at it separately.

Let's start by considering what punctuation does. An old word for 'to punctuate' was 'to point' and that's a useful way to think of punctuation: a means of pointing out what belongs to what in a sentence. When the pointing goes wrong you can send readers down completely the wrong path, so it's critical to get it right.

In a moment we're going to look at each punctuation mark in turn. Before we do, though, be aware that there's a growing trend towards minimising punctuation. For example, if you're of a certain age you may have been taught to put semicolons at the end of items in a bulleted list, and full stops (periods) after the last item. Nowadays this convention is considered fussy and old-fashioned and so best avoided. Similarly, you no longer need dots in abbreviations such as *eg* and *ie*. I've had people almost come to blows with me when I've removed their dots, but have a look at the style guides for modern respectable publications and they'll usually favour no dots. Also, be aware that some punctuation rules are culturally specific, such as whether to put the comma inside or outside quotation marks (US English – always inside; UK English – outside if the quote is incomplete). Whatever conventions you adopt, the two most important things are to be consistent and to consider your readership (eg US v UK).

Right, time now to examine each major punctuation mark in turn, starting with the comma as it probably causes more confusion than any other punctuation mark.

Commas

Why's the little comma, the tadpole of punctuation, such a slippery creature? Perhaps because it's freer than other punctuation marks to swim where it will, so it often wriggles into the wrong place or swims away when it's needed.

One of the commonest comma issues relates to restrictive v nonrestrictive clauses. If you're not familiar with these terms, don't worry because we'll get to that in a moment. For now, see if you can spot how the presence or absence of a comma changes the following sentence's meaning:

1 Sales are handled by the UK teams which are in London
2 Sales are handled by the UK teams, which are in London

Sentence 1 is saying that of the UK teams, the only ones that handle sales are those in London. The meaning of 'UK teams' is being *restricted* to 'in London' – so the clause 'which are in London' is *restrictive*. In sentence 2, adding the comma removes the restriction: what the sentence now says is that sales are handled by the UK teams, and (incidental information – *nonrestrictive*) those teams happen to be in London.

Look back at the two examples above and you'll see that they both contain the word *which*. There's an old rule (better preserved in the US than the UK) about using *that* for restrictive clauses and *which* for nonrestrictive clauses, but generally *which* is OK for either. What's definitely wrong is using *that* for a nonrestrictive clause:

✗ Sales are handled by the UK teams, *that* are in London

But the best solution for restrictive clauses is often simply to delete *which/that* altogether:

✓ Sales are handled by the UK teams ~~that are~~ in London

The comma issue most likely to cause heated debate is whether to add a comma before the final *and/or* in a list (what's known as a 'serial comma' or 'Oxford comma'). What matters is clarity, as in the following two examples where an Oxford comma is essential:

✗ I met the bishops of Canterbury, Durham and Bath and Wells
✓ I met the bishops of Canterbury, Durham, and Bath and Wells
✗ I'd like to thank my parents, Mother Theresa and God *[could be misread as, 'I'd like to thank my mum who's Mother Theresa and my dad who's God']*
✓ I'd like to thank my parents, Mother Theresa, and God

One supposed 'rule' for the Oxford comma is that you should always use it when three items or more are listed – but this rule's misleadingly simplistic. First, a comma can actually be useful when you have only two items. For example:

? Plasma is a hot gas comprising positively charged ions and electrons

Here, a physicist would know instantly that electrons are negative and so realise that 'positively charged' applies only to ions and not electrons – but less scientific readers might puzzle over whether it applies to both. Adding an Oxford comma removes the ambiguity, although another fix is to change the word order:

✓ (Oxford comma) Plasma is a hot gas comprising positively charged ions, and electrons.
✓ (Reordering the words) Plasma is a hot gas comprising electrons and positively charged ions.

Second, when a sentence has no risk of ambiguity whatsoever, a gratuitous Oxford comma looks pedantic and silly, and merely adds visual clutter:

✗ The three colours of the Union Jack are red, white, and blue.
✓ The three colours of the Union Jack are red, white and blue.

A further problem with the supposed 'rule' of always using an Oxford comma for three items or more is that an Oxford comma can falsely suggest that restrictive clauses (which we looked at earlier) apply only to the final item in a list instead of all of them. To understand this problem, have a look at the following phrase that appeared on a Brexit-themed 50-pence coin issued in January 2020:

Peace, prosperity and friendship with all nations

This phrase caused a furore, not because of the sentiment expressed but because it didn't have an Oxford comma. People with entrenched positions on both sides were missing the most important point, namely *what meaning was intended*:

- No Oxford comma suggests [Peace, prosperity and friendship] with all nations.
- Oxford comma suggests [Peace, prosperity], and friendship with all nations.

Let's look a little deeper at this nuance, using the kind of example you might come across in a business document. Suppose you want to make three recommendations for reducing the risk of fraud:

✗ We recommend you upgrade your software, enhance your security checks, and insource your call centre to reduce the risk of fraud

With the Oxford comma the sentence appears to say: 'We recommend you upgrade your software, enhance your security checks, [and insource your call centre to reduce the risk of fraud]' – giving the misleading impression that only the final recommendation applies to reducing the risk of fraud.

Removing the Oxford comma reduces the ambiguity by loosening the tie between 'reduce the risk of fraud' and the final recommendation. But the sentence still shimmers with ambiguity:

- We recommend you upgrade your software, enhance your security checks and insource your call centre to reduce the risk of fraud

The way to remove the ambiguity altogether is to shift the restrictive clause to the front of the list:

✓ *To reduce the risk of fraud*, we recommend you upgrade your software, enhance your security checks and insource your call centre *[Oxford comma optional]*

Be aware that adding or removing a comma before a 'joining' word such as *and* or *or* (what are called 'conjunctions' or 'coordinators') can radically change a sentence's meaning. Take the following two sentences, which are identical apart from the second one having a comma added before *and*:

- The new legislation applies to trades between UK businesses and EU countries
- The new legislation applies to trades between UK businesses, and EU countries

Without the comma, the sentence is saying is that the new legislation applies to one thing only: trading between UK businesses and the EU. But with the comma it's saying that the new legislation applies to two things: trades between UK businesses, and to the EU as well.

Finally, if you're unhappy with your sentence both with and without the Oxford comma, you have a third option and that's to drop *and*. A further advantage is that doing so can make your sentence more dramatic. Let's say you've written:

- We'll help you to build your products, expand your markets and develop new revenue streams

It's not a bad sentence – but you think it sounds a bit bland, and you're not sure whether to add that Oxford comma. Now compare it with:

✓ We'll help you to build your products, to expand your markets, to develop new revenue streams

Sounds grander, doesn't it? In fact, by removing the connective word *and* we've employed a rhetorical device called 'asyndeton' that's often used by orators and by writers wanting to create a sense of drama: think of Churchill's famous 'We shall fight on the beaches' speech and the famous quote attributed to Julius Caesar, 'I came, I saw, I conquered.' But because of the potential for grandeur, be careful not to overuse asyndeta or you risk sounding overblown.

Yet another approach, much favoured by advertising copywriters, is using super-short sentences (or sentence fragments):

✓ We'll help you to build your products. Expand your markets. Develop new revenue streams.

But even more so than using asyndeta, this approach works best when used in moderation – and only then when it suits the context. Short ad copy? Fine. For anything else, though, go easy or your text will sound too choppy.

Another comma problem is that missing or misplaced commas can create a garden-path sentence (those sentences, which we looked at earlier, that lead you up the garden path into a false reading):

✗ As with other elements of the calculation testing is also performed *['As with other elements of the calculation testing … is also performed'? Huh?]*

✓ As with other elements of the calculation, testing is also performed

A trick for placing commas correctly is to notice if and where you take a pause when saying the sentence. Try it with the following pair of sentences:

✓ Let's eat, Grandma! *[Grandma's being invited to enjoy her meal]*
✗ Let's eat Grandma! *[Grandma's going to be eaten]*

Similarly, compare the difference between:

✓ I know, John *[you're saying 'I know' to a person called John]*
✓ I know John *[you're saying you know who John is]*

A missing comma can also leave readers wondering how to parse a sentence:

? Other expenses are paid for by ABC and XYZ and ABC's share is therefore included in ABC's own expense basis

Does this mean that other expenses are paid for by [ABC and XYZ] or by [ABC]? Look how the position of the added comma in each of the following examples clarifies which meaning was meant:

✓ Other expenses are paid for by ABC, and XYZ and ABC's share is therefore included in ABC's own expense basis
✓ Other expenses are paid for by ABC and XYZ, and ABC's share is therefore included in ABC's own expense basis

Here's another example of how awkwardly placed commas make it hard to parse a sentence:

✗ This legal entity complies with the risk-calibration framework, *as evidenced by its calibration papers and with the capital reserves manual*, as evidenced by its sign-off document

Reposition the commas and the logic of the sentence becomes clear:

✓ This legal entity complies with the risk-calibration framework as evidenced by its calibration papers, *and with the capital reserves manual as evidenced by its sign-off document*

A comma or its absence can even change a word's meaning:

- However you want to do this *[however = 'in whatever way']*
- However, you want to do this *[however = 'nevertheless']*

It can also change a word's emotional tone:

- Please call me *[polite request]*
- Please, call me *[begging]*
- Get out! *[either panic or 'hot' anger]*
- Get. Out. *['cold' anger – and a good example of how 'wrong' punctuation can be right, if you know how and why to break the rules]*

Another big comma issue is missing parenthetical commas. What does this mean? Well, a parenthesis is either supplementary information bracketed off within a sentence or the round brackets () themselves – and just as brackets need to be paired to enclose the parenthesis at both ends, so too do commas:

✗ In this sentence, illustrating parentheses the closing comma is missing
✓ In this sentence, illustrating parentheses, the closing comma is present

To test if words are parenthetical, remove them and see if the sentence still makes sense. Or listen to how you say the sentence, and you'll notice how you naturally pause slightly before and after the parenthesis. Try it now with the following examples, noticing how the meaning changes depending on whether there's a parenthesis:

- The CEO, said the regulator, was to blame *[regulator is blaming CEO]*
- The CEO said the regulator was to blame *[CEO is blaming regulator]*

This sense-test of removing the parenthetical words to see what's left also shows why one of these sentences works but the other doesn't:

✓ The first Roman emperor, Augustus, transformed the Roman republic to an empire following the assassination of his great-uncle, Julius Caesar
✗ Software engineer, John Smith, worked at IBM

… and why these two fixes work:

✓ Software engineer John Smith worked at IBM
✓ John Smith, a software engineer, worked at IBM

It's sometimes OK to use a comma after a parenthesis in brackets, but never before and after:

✗ After oversleeping, (forgetting to set my alarm), I missed my train

Again, sense-check by removing the parenthetical words and brackets. When you do so, you'll see that what you're left with, and what's noticeably wrong, is two consecutive commas:

✗ After oversleeping,, I missed my train

Also note that a single comma goes *after* the bracketed parenthesis and not before:

✗ After oversleeping, (forgetting to set my alarm) I missed my train
✓ After oversleeping (forgetting to set my alarm), I missed my train

This time, removing the parenthetical words and brackets shows why it was right to have just the one comma:

✓ After oversleeping, I missed my train

Here's another subtlety involving parentheses. In the first sentence, the verb is plural because the subject of the sentence is all three people who won the Nobel Prize:

✓ In December 1903, Marie Curie, Pierre Curie and Henri Becquerel *were* awarded the Nobel Prize in Physics

But if we put parentheses around the two winners other than Marie Curie, the subject is now Marie Curie alone and the verb becomes singular:

✓ In December 1903, Marie Curie (and Pierre Curie and Henri Becquerel) *was* awarded the Nobel Prize in Physics

Again, we're applying the principle of removing the bracketed words to see what's left.

As well as using commas or curly brackets to enclose a parenthesis, you can also use dashes – the best choice if you want to emphasise the parenthesis, because dashes separate the text more visibly than either commas or brackets:

- Only one option (upgrading to the latest release) will solve this software issue
- Only one option – upgrading to the latest release – will solve this software issue

  One nerdy aside about dashes is that they come in two sizes, en and em, so called because traditionally they were the widths of the letters N and M respectively, with the en dash half the length of the em (although nowadays about the only rule that holds is that em dashes are noticeably longer than en dashes). In the UK, it's more typical to use en dashes with spaces either side, while the US convention is em dashes without spaces:

- (UK) Only one option – upgrading to the latest release – will solve this software issue
- (US) Only one option—upgrading to the latest release—will solve this software issue

Also note that a dash is not the same as a hyphen, hyphens being noticeably shorter and slightly fatter than either en or em dashes (- – —).

When the parenthetical text itself contains commas, for clarity it's best to stick to round brackets or dashes to avoid confusion:

✗ Three options, upgrading, replacing or reconfiguring, are available for fixing the software
✓ Three options (upgrading, replacing or reconfiguring) are available for fixing the software
✓ Three options – upgrading, replacing or reconfiguring – are available for fixing the software

… but in such cases it's often easier on your readers if you move the parenthetical information to the end, prefixed by a colon:

✓ Three options are available for fixing the software: *upgrading, replacing or reconfiguring*

The final thing to note about commas is 'comma splicing', which means separating sentences with a comma. Comma splicing isn't necessarily wrong. Take 'I came, I saw, I conquered,' which we looked at earlier as an example of asyndeton (dropping conjunctions) – it can be read as a single sentence with the conjunction *and* removed, but equally as three short sentences separated by commas.

The reason it works both ways is that all three sentences are simple and they're conceptually coherent. The moment you start trying to connect disjointed sentences with a comma is when you run into trouble:

✗ The development team reviews bugs, they review them every day.

Let your ear be the judge. With the example above, you'll hear a rushed quality because the pause after 'bugs' is too short. In fact, one of the commonest (deliberate) uses of comma splicing is when novelists want to dialogue to sound rushed and breathless:

✓ 'Dave's like, whatever, so me and Chantelle we went to the pub, we had like ten Jägerbombs and got totally bladdered, yeah?'

And you don't want your business writing to sound like that, do you?

Back to that 'reviews bugs, they review them' sentence – the way to fix it is either to change the comma to a full stop or (more elegantly) to cut the extra words:

✓ The development team reviews bugs every day.

'Run-on sentences' are like comma splices except with no punctuation at all separating the sentences. Unlike comma splicing, run-on sentences are never right:

✗ I came I saw I conquered.

The fixes are the same as for comma splicing.

Hyphens

Along with commas, hyphens are the trickiest punctuation mark so take a deep breath and prepare yourself for a longish read. It's worth it, though, because of the gains you'll make in clarity.

A useful way to think of hyphens is as little rivets welding words into a single unit of meaning. Thinking of them like this will help you spot where a missing hyphen's changed your meaning. For example:

- *single-premium bonds* are bonds that have only one premium, but *single premium bonds* are premium bonds of which there is only one instance.
- *30-minute intervals* are intervals of 30 minutes, but *30 minute intervals* means 30 intervals of 1 minute – or even 30 tiny intervals, if you pronounce 'minute' with long vowels.
- *man-eating tigers* are tigers that eat men, but a *man eating tigers* is a very brave and hungry man.

You don't hyphenate when proper nouns are involved (names of specific things or people – *Microsoft*, *Tuesday*, *Fred*) as they're capitalised and hence clearly seen as forming a single semantic unit:

✓ North American firms

Such bolted-together qualifiers are called 'compound modifiers'. Here's another example:

✓ Red and blue flags = red-only flags and blue-only flags
✓ Red-and-blue flags = bicoloured flags

In the following examples, the absence of a hyphen leaves a phrase's meaning hovering between two interpretations:

✗ client support team:

 ? Team for supporting clients, or client's own support team?
 ✓ client-support team (first meaning) or client's support team (second meaning)

✗ key risk mitigation techniques

 ? Key techniques for mitigating risks, or techniques for mitigating key risks?
 ✓ key risk-mitigation techniques or key-risk mitigation techniques

Then you have what are called 'suspended hyphens', where one or more compound modifiers are held in suspension till the final one:

✓ The train company provides *first-* and second-class carriages but their service is decidedly third class

And notice how the presence or absence of a suspended hyphen modifies meaning:

- medium and long-tail risks (medium risks and long-tail risks)
- medium- and long-tail risks (medium-tail and long-tail risks)

If there's no risk of ambiguity and the hyphen looks ugly, it's OK to leave it out. But if in doubt hyphenate, because clarity trumps aesthetics.

If compound modifiers come *after* the thing they modify, don't use hyphens if they're modifying a verb but use personal preference if they're modifying a noun or pronoun:

✓ She inched *step by step* towards the exit *['inched' is a verb, so no hyphens]*
✓ She is *happy go lucky / happy-go-lucky ['she' is a pronoun, so hyphens optional]*

My personal preference is never to use hyphens when the modifier comes after, because it keeps the rule simple and because I feel that avoiding unnecessary hyphens makes text look tidier. But, as I say, it's only a personal preference.

If you find yourself with a distracting string-of-pearls effect of excessive hyphenation, one way round the problem is to use apostrophes:

✗ Each *legal-entity* internal-model validation …
✓ Each *legal entity's* internal-model validation …

Apostrophes can be very useful for breaking the monotony of what's known as 'noun-banging' – stacking nouns together in complex and hard-to-understand phrases such as 'system interface software methodology tools'. And as well as breaking the monotony, apostrophes can remove ambiguity:

? Mega Corp *Group* Vendor Management Office
✓ *Mega Corp Group's* Vendor Management Office
✓ Mega Corp's *Group Vendor Management Office*

These examples of noun-banging illustrate what are called 'noun adjuncts' – nouns functioning as adjectives. Noun adjuncts explain why you can write things such as *the system interface* and *your phone number* rather than having to use possessives (*system's interface, your phone's number*). Noun adjuncts tend to be singular, with the plural forms risking looking like a mistake: eg if you wrote *systems interface*, readers might assume you'd dropped an apostrophe.

A second way to avoid excessive hyphenation is quotation marks, which are especially useful for phrases that would otherwise require two or more hyphens:

✓ This is the basis for valuing 'on balance sheet' liabilities.

A final way to avoid too many hyphens is reordering the words:

✗ long term capital and liquidity profiles
  ? [long term capital] and [liquidity] profiles
  ? [long term] [capital and liquidity] profiles
✓ Long-term-capital and liquidity profiles *[correct but clunky]*
✓ Profiles for long-term capital and liquidity *[correct and elegant]*

Although the more common mistake with compound modifiers is leaving out the hyphen, it's also a mistake (and confusing for readers) to add a hyphen that creates a false compound modifier:

✗ zero-data loss *[loss of data categorised as 'zero']*
✓ zero data loss *[no data lost]*

A final point to note about hyphens and compound modifiers is that separate words often fuse over time if they form a single concept. For example, the word *today* used to be written as *to day*, before becoming *to-day* and finally *today*. More recently, we've seen *e-mail* almost universally settle on *email*, with *website* lagging slightly behind as it's still often written as *web site*. So which do you choose: two words, hyphenated, or one word? It's especially tricky when deciding whether to hyphenate prefixes. The *Economist's* style guide, for example, recommends *non-existent* but also *nonstop*, so do you write *non-financial* or *nonfinancial*?

Let legibility guide your decisions: I tend to misread *coworker* as *cow-orker*, so I prefer *co-worker*, but maybe that's just me. Less subjective are words starting with *re-* that need hyphenating to avoid confusion with what the word means without the hyphen, eg *re-sign/resign*, *re-form/reform* and *re-sent/resent*. Ditto a hyphen to avoid *co-op* being misread (and mispronounced) as *coop*.

The States tends to be slightly ahead of the UK in terms of welding words into one. Is it that notorious British reserve, wanting words to keep their distance with a space or a hyphen like a privet hedge? I don't know, but I'm with the Americans on this one. For instance, it niggles me that 'cash flow' is still generally considered two words when to my mind (and eye) they so obviously form a single semantic unit. And keeping the words separate makes for messy hyphenation when the words become adjectival: compare, for example, the compact elegance of 'non-cashflow results' with the word-necklace of 'non-cash-flow results'.

Also, joining words helps readers grasp a concept as a semantic unity (eg *webpage*) and enables constructions such as *(non)financial*. It can also help reduce ambiguities caused by a verb being misread as a noun – remember our earlier 'Save soap and waste paper' example and how we could eliminate the misreading by writing *wastepaper* as one word?

The main point is that whatever choices you make (eg *web site* or *website*) you apply them consistently. One area where the decision whether to hyphenate is much more straightforward is after adverbs ending in *-ly*, when you never need a hyphen. A hyphen's suspect when the *-ly* adverb forms part of a compound modifier and downright wrong when it doesn't. Your safest option is total avoidance:

✓ strongly worded letter
? strongly-worded letter
✓ a letter that was strongly worded
✗ a letter that was strongly-worded

A final and very specific point to note about hyphens is that on rare occasions they can be misread as minus signs, or vice versa:

? *AA-* rated companies *[AA- rating, or AA rating where the author's accidentally included a space?]*

To remove the ambiguity, you need to reorder the words so they can't be read as involving a hyphen. In other words, depending on which meaning is intended:

✓ (*either*) Companies with an AA- rating
✓ (*or*) Companies with an AA rating

Here's another example, where Microsoft Word has auto-replaced the minus sign with a dash, compounding the risk of misreading:

? This approach would result in profits being recognised on the simple basis of charges – expenses
✓ This approach would result in profits being recognised on the simple basis of charges *less* expenses

Apostrophes

Some people are scared by apostrophes, but apostrophes have only three uses of which the third is relatively rare. So they're not *that* scary, although there are some quirks you need to know about. Let's start with the commonest use, which is to mark possession. For example, rather than having to write the *bone belonging to Fido* or *the bone of Fido*, we can write *Fido's bone* – that's marking possession.

The general rule is that possessive apostrophes go before the *s* for singular nouns and irregular plurals (ie plurals not formed by adding *-s*); but after the *s* for regular plurals:

✓ manager's report *[report from one manager]*
✓ managers' report *[report from several managers]*
✓ men's, women's and children's clothes *[irregular plurals, so apostrophe before s]*

Never put an apostrophe in a plural word if there's no possession (an error known as the greengrocer's apostrophe):

✗ Fresh banana's and homegrown tomato's
✓ Fresh bananas and homegrown tomatoes

Singular possession usually needs the final *s*, even when the noun ends in an *s*:

✗ The *status'* end date
✓ The *status's* end date *[but statuses' if plural]*

Exceptions do exist, eg while St James's Park in London is spelt and punctuated as expected, Newcastle United's football ground is St James' Park and Exeter City's is St James Park. If in doubt, check a reliable source such as:

www.lexico.com/grammar/apostrophe

It's perhaps because of such quirky exceptions that many people try to avoid apostrophes altogether. For example, rather than writing *the system's interface* they'll write *the system interface* or (more clumsily) *the interface of the system*. The danger of doing so is that you can create an ambiguity that an apostrophe would have avoided. Take the following sentence, where it's unclear what the phrase 'of the company' is applying to, and how repositioning the phrase and adding an apostrophe shows which meaning is meant:

? The target is set considering the current business plan and capital requirements of the company

✓ The target is set considering the company's current business plan and capital requirements

✓ The target is set considering the current business plan and the company's capital requirements

Finally, if you're a grammar geek here's an interesting fact for you: the apostrophe for possessive nouns is, historically, an instance of indicating a missing letter (the second major use of apostrophes, which we'll look at next). In Anglo-Saxon English, the genitive case was indicated by the ending *-es*, eg Johnes book.

After marking possession, the next major use of apostrophes is to mark missing letters. For example, *o'clock* was originally the phrase *of the clock* and *fo'c'sle* comes from *forecastle*. Sometimes the apostrophe withers over time, eg *All Hallows' Eve* shrank to *Hallowe'en* then further shrank to *Halloween*.

Hallowe'en reminds us of these two major functions of the apostrophe, showing missing letters and showing possessives (although admittedly the apostrophe is in the wrong place for *Hallows'*). And it's muddling these two functions that causes one of the commonest punctuation errors in the entire English language, namely writing *it's* (*it is*) when you mean the possessive pronoun *its*, hence:

✗ The gun was in *it's* box (and an enraged pedant shot me)

✓ The gun was in *its* box (and the grammar doctor smiled)

To remember the difference, say to yourself, 'It's *his, her, its* and not *hi's, he'r, it's*.' The *only* possessive pronoun with an apostrophe is *one's* (don't ask why, it just is) – hence *his, her, its, mine, ours, yours, theirs*.

The final and comparatively rare use of apostrophes is to clarify ambiguous plurals, eg *dotting the i's and crossing the t's* or *He got A's in his exams.* Where there's no ambiguity, don't use apostrophes: *Mind your Ps and Qs.*

You don't use apostrophes for plurals of acronyms (words formed from initial letters, eg radar) and initialisms (initials that don't form a word, eg PDF), except for the usual reasons of indicating possession or missing letters:

✗ The PDF's are on the shared drive
✓ The PDFs are on the shared drive
✓ The PDF's *[PDF is]* on the shared drive

✗ CEO's and CTO's attended the conference
✓ CEOs and CTOs attended the conference

✓ We met at the CTO's dinner *[single CTO, so presumably a dinner hosted by a CTO]*
✓ We met at the CTOs' dinner *[multiple CTOs, so presumably a dinner for CTOs]*

Quotation marks

The rules for quotation marks are simple: either single quotes (' ') or double quotes (" ") throughout, the only exception being nested quotes where you use the opposite (doubles instead of singles, or vice versa) for contrast:

✓ 'As Socrates reminds us,' said John, '"An unexamined life is not worth living."'
✓ "As Socrates reminds us," said John, "'An unexamined life is not worth living.'"

US English tends to favour double quotes and UK English singles, but there's no hard rule on which to choose – what counts is consistency. But one factor worth considering is that double quotes can sometimes help to avoid confusion between quotes and apostrophes:

? He said, 'Parents' behaviour affects children.'
✓ He said, "Parents' behaviour affects children."

Avoid using quotation marks to emphasise words, unless you intend an element of doubt or irony (when used this way they're called *distance quotes*, and for a reason):

✗ Our company offers the 'best' solution *[sounds sarcastic]*
✓ Our company offers the best solution

If you have a question mark or exclamation mark just before a closing quote, don't add a full stop (period) after the quote. Both question and exclamation marks close a sentence just as a full stop does, so adding a full stop afterwards is as wrong as finishing a sentence with two full stops. For example, just as you would never write:

✗ She said, 'I am going to the party.'.

Equally, you must never write:

✗ She said, 'Are you coming to the party?'.

Instead you write:

✓ She said, 'Are you coming to the party?'

And finally, be aware that the symbols for feet and inches, and minutes and seconds of an angle, are *never* curly quotes. They actually have their own symbols that are like forward-sloping straight quotes, hence:

- Six feet two inches is *not* 6'2" – it is 6′2″
- An angle of 60 degrees, 40 minutes and 20 seconds is *not* 60°40'20' – it is 60°40′20″

Ampersands

Use an ampersand (&) only when it's part of a company's name or an accepted abbreviation, eg *R&D*. In other circumstances, it's usually preferable to write *and* as a word.

Exclamation marks

Use exclamation marks extremely sparingly, if at all. Their purpose (the clue's in the name) is to exclaim. 'Help!' is justified but, unless you're an overexcited child, not 'We had pizza on Tuesday!'

This capacity of exclamation marks to trivialise is beautifully illustrated by the following example, which I've borrowed from the book *Newspaper Language* by Nicholas Bagnall. Imagine reading the following two headlines:

DISASTER
DISASTER!

You'd assume the first is a genuine disaster, perhaps a plane crash or some other tragedy in which people have died, but you'd rarely do the same with the second one. Instead, you're more likely to assume it's something trivial such as, 'Disaster! We invited our new neighbours to dinner and everyone's soufflé collapsed!'

It's this potential for a shrill, overexcited quality that explains why many editors call exclamation marks 'shrieks' or 'screamers'. F Scott Fitzgerald said that using them is like laughing at your own jokes – a charge that can be aimed at emoticons and emojis as well. After all, if you need to add a smiley face to *tell* someone you've made a joke, was it really that funny in the first place?

And in a business context, never, ever use more than one shriek in a row. Because, like, ohmigod!!! It looks sooo, like, childish!!!

Question marks

Question marks are for marking questions – direct questions, that is, not indirect ones:

✓ Are you going to the pub after work?
✗ Raj asked if you're going to the pub after work?

Similarly, suppositions don't merit a question mark:

✓ Are you sure you want to do that?
✗ Surely you don't want to do that? *[= I'm sure you don't want to do that]*

Colons and semicolons

The first thing to note about colons (:) and semicolons (;) is that they provide a softer break between sentences than full stops, and the difference between the two is subtle but effective. Strictly speaking, when sentences are separated by anything other than a full stop, exclamation mark or question mark, they become what are called main (or independent) clauses, meaning parts of a sentence that could function as sentences in their own right. But if it's easier, you can just think of them as sentences that happen to be joined by some other punctuation.

Compare:

✓ (full stop) Here is one idea. Here is another idea.
✓ (semicolon) Here is an idea; here is a closely related idea.
✓ (colon) Here is an idea: and here is the answer or fulfilment of that idea.

Sam Leith, in *Write to the Point*, has a lovely way of describing the colon's function as being to staple two things together: the two dots of a colon even look like the punch marks of a staple, don't they?

One quirk about the colon is that in the UK the first letter after the colon always follows normal capitalisation rules, whereas in the United States it's sometimes capitalised if what follows the colon forms a complete sentence:

✓ (UK – always) This bit forms a full sentence: *this* bit forms a full sentence as well.

✓ (US – sometimes) This bit forms a full sentence: *This* bit forms a full sentence as well.

As for the semicolon, some people consider it a bit old-fashioned and suggest using a dash instead. In fact, you could use a dash in all three of the 'full stop v semicolon v colon' examples I gave above and many writers do:

- Here is one idea – here is another idea.
- Here is an idea – here is a closely related idea.
- Here is an idea – here is the answer or fulfilment of that idea.

But it's a shame to lose those subtle shades of meaning between the three, don't you think? Also, too many dashes can become visually distracting, giving a chopped-up look to your prose. Where dashes *are* effective is stretching a single sentence with a dramatic pause – like this. Contrast this stretching effect with using a full stop instead, which creates the sense of an afterthought. Like that.

The final thing to note about colons and semicolons is that the correct punctuation mark for introducing lists is a colon (:) not a semicolon (;).

CHECK YOUR GRAMMAR

Let's turn now to common grammatical errors and how to fix them.

Creating subject-verb disagreements

'Subject-verb agreement' is the rule that singular subjects need singular verbs, and plural subjects need plural verbs. Here are some typical agreement errors, along with explanations as to what's gone wrong:

✗ The rationale for model changes ~~are~~ is reported

The writer's mistaken the word just before the verb (*changes*) as the subject, seen it's plural and so made the verb plural – but the true subject is *rationale*, at the start of the sentence.

✗ The latest log summarising all of the weaknesses and limitations of the internal model ~~*are*~~ <u>*is*</u> stored on SharePoint

The same problem as in the previous example in that the true subject (*log*) is at the start of the sentence, but the error's even trickier to spot because of there being not one but two plural nouns just before the verb.

✗ All message attributes are human-readable text that ~~*are*~~ <u>*is*</u> displayed on the user interface

The writer's mentally skipped 'human-readable text' and read the sentence as 'All message attributes ~~are human-readable text~~ are displayed' and hence failed to see that the second verb should be agreeing with 'text'. A more elegant fix than changing 'text that are' to 'text that is' would be to cut *that is*:

All message attributes are human-readable text ~~*that is*~~ displayed on the user interface

✗ The calibration and methodology ~~*is*~~ <u>*are*</u> described in the pricing manual

The two singulars (*calibration* and *methodology*) make a plural, just as with the sentence 'My dog and cat *are* always fighting.' The writer's confusion here is in treating 'calibration and methodology' as if they formed a single concept, in which case singular would be right. Compare with 'The ship's constant rolling, pitching and yawing in the storm *was* making me seasick.'

An *either/neither* sentence with a single subject is singular:

✓ Either day *is* fine
✓ Neither option *is* acceptable

With *either/or* and *neither/nor* sentences, however, the verb's singular when both subjects are singular and plural when both are plural:

✓ Either a cheque or a BACS transfer *is* acceptable
✓ Neither knives nor scissors with blades of 6 cm or more *are* allowed in hand luggage

Such sentences only get tricky if one subject's singular and one's plural:

? Either Fred or his brothers [*is/are*?] coming

Some authorities state that plural always takes preference, others that it depends on which subject's closest to the verb (what's called the proximity rule). In the above example, both rules are satisfied by Fred (singular) coming before brothers (plural) so *are* is the right choice:

✓ Either Fred or his brothers *are* coming

But if you can avoid the singular/plural imbalance, do so because it sounds better:

? Either beer or wines are available
✓ Either beer or wine is available

Creating hanging modifiers

'Hanging modifiers' (aka hanging/dangling participles) are words or phrases modifying something that's missing from the sentence. Here's a classic example:

✗ As a highly valued customer, *we* …

It's not we (the company) who is 'a highly valued customer' but the customer:

✓ As *you are* a highly valued customer, we …

Similarly:

✗ Walking down the street, *the flowers* were beautiful *[the flowers aren't walking]*
✓ Walking down the street, *I noticed that* the flowers were beautiful
✗ *Shared drives* gain storage space by deleting unnecessary files *[the drives aren't deleting files]*
✓ (either) Shared drives gain storage space *when users delete* unnecessary files
✓ (or) Shared drives gain storage space when unnecessary files are deleted

Hanging modifiers can also occur if you're missing one of a pair of parenthetical commas (which, you may remember, are commas bracketing off information nested inside a sentence):

✗ On high-stress days, researchers have found that we overgeneralise

What the sentence is saying, incorrectly, is that when *researchers* are stressed, they find that people overgeneralise. To fix the problem, you've two options:

✓ (add the missing parenthetical comma) On high-stress days, researchers have found, people overgeneralise
✓ (rephrase) Researchers have found that people overgeneralise on high-stress days

Treating plural abbreviations as singular

If an abbreviation is plural, write it as such. For example, the plural of 'interest rate swap' is 'interest rate swaps' and the same is true when it's abbreviated to IRS:

✗ The IRS page contains all *IRS* known to the price engine
✓ The IRS price page contains all *IRSs* known to the price engine

And, please, no apostrophe (*IRS's*) unless it's a possessive singular:

✓ The *IRS's* settlement date

Using plurals for mass nouns

A mass noun (aka uncountable noun) is a noun describing something that can't be counted, eg *information* or *furniture*. Mass nouns are always singular, eg you can't write *informations* or *furnitures*; and they can't take an indefinite article (*a* or *an*), eg you can't write *an information*. Therefore, watch out for errors such as:

✗ *A nonsense* (the test being that you can't have *nonsenses*)
✗ *Trainings* (the test being that you can't have *a training*)
? *Behaviours* (some dictionaries list it, but careful readers may prefer a construction such as *forms of behaviour*)

And note that the convention in standard English is to use 'fewer' for countable nouns and 'less' for uncountable nouns:

✓ Global warming is leading to *less* ice and *fewer* polar bears.

Writing 'comprises of'

'Comprises' means 'consists of', so *comprises of* and *comprised of* are wrong:

- Basic own funds comprise ~~*of*~~ the excess of assets over liabilities.

Confusing I, me and myself

I, *me* and *myself* are often muddled. The correct usages are as follows:

- I = subject: 'I ate breakfast'
- Me = object: 'It happened to me'
- Myself = reflexive or emphatic: reflexive means that the pronoun *reflects* back on the subject ('I cut *myself*') while emphatic means that

the pronoun adds emphasis ('Jane wrote the document *herself*'). In both cases, the pronoun agrees with the subject or object (I/myself, you/yourself, etc)

Here are some examples of common *I/me/myself* errors, along with explanations as to what's gone wrong:

✗ Between you and *I*

The usual argument against this usage is that you wouldn't say 'between *we*' but 'between *us*' so the phrase should be 'between you and *me*'. Some respected linguists say this line of argument's fallacious, but most authorities (including the Oxford English Dictionary) state that the construction's wrong. As the only thing to be gained by writing 'between you and I' is the ire of some readers, it's best to stick with 'between you and me'.

✗ Talk to your manager and *I*

Remove the other person and the sentence becomes 'Talk to I' – showing that the correct form is 'Talk to your manager and *me*.'

✗ *Me* [or *Myself*] and John went to the pub

Again, the test of removing the other person shows that *me* is wrong in this context because with standard English you'd never write '*Me* went to the pub' – the correct forms are either 'John and *I* went to the pub' or '*I* went to the pub *myself*'.

(I say '*standard* English' because in some dialects 'Me and John went' would be accepted, as indeed would 'Me went to the pub' – a formation that occurs in Jamaican patois. The point here is that we're looking at formal written English, for which only the 'John and I' formation is considered correct.)

Also note that in polite speech and writing you put the other person before yourself, hence 'John and I' rather than 'I and John'.

✗ For bookings, please talk to *myself*

Unless I suffer from a multiple-personality disorder, the only person who can 'talk to myself' is me – so the correct form is 'For bookings, please talk to *me*.'

Using that *instead of* who

Never say *that* for people in contexts where the word *who* would fit. Sometimes *who* doesn't fit: you couldn't, for instance, change '*That* guy works in sales' to '*Who* guy works in sales'. But in all those instances where *who* does fit, the rule is *who* for people and *that* for things:

- The system *that* logs complaints is being replaced
- The person ~~*that*~~ *who* deals with complaints is Joe Smith

When the person is the object of the sentence, it gets trickier because *whom* is technically correct but can sound stuffy (and the *who/whom* distinction is gradually being lost in modern usage) – so the neatest solution is to use no word at all:

✗ The person ~~*that*~~ *whom* I appointed
✓ The person ~~*whom*~~ I appointed

Confusing Latin abbreviations

If you use Latin abbreviations, make sure you use them correctly. On several occasions I've seen writers confusing *ie* (which means 'namely') with *eg* (which means 'for example'). Another common error is to append *etc* onto a sentence where it's not needed. Since *etc* means 'and so on', it's redundant (and bad style) to combine it with *eg*, *such as*, *for instance* and similar phrases; one or the other suffices:

✗ We investigated operational risks *such as* data breaches, fraud, human error, *etc*
✓ We investigated operational risks *such as* data breaches, fraud *and* human error

Latin abbreviations can confuse even native English readers, so you're best off using English alternatives for anything other than the best known (*eg*, *ie*, *etc*). For example, if you wanted a Latin abbreviation for 'compare with' would you know the difference between *cf* and *qv*? Well into my career as a writer I didn't even know of *qv*, until to my embarrassment a colleague (who wasn't a writer) pointed out that I was using *cf* for *qv*. If I'd stuck to the English expression I'd have been fine.

Confusing 'due to' and 'because of'

The phrase 'due to' applies to nouns while 'because of' applies to verbs. This distinction is falling into disuse, but – as Sam Leith observes in his book *Write to the Point* – it's worth knowing if your ear's telling you a sentence sounds odd and you're not sure why:

- The *failure* was ~~*because of*~~ *due to* bugs in the software
- The system *failed* ~~*due to*~~ *because of* bugs in the software

Repeating or missing words after abbreviations

Avoid adding a word after an initialism or acronym that already contains the word. For example, since 'pin' stands for 'personal identification number' it's redundant to write 'pin number'. Similarly, make sure you add words where they're needed. For example, in everyday conversation British people will say, 'My car passed its MOT' – but as MOT stands for 'Ministry of Transport', in more formal written contexts it's better to write 'MOT *test*'.

Choosing the wrong word (eg homophones)

'Homophones' are words pronounced the same way but spelt differently (*to/too*, *their/there*, *your/you're*, etc). It's easy to type the wrong one, particularly if you're 'hearing' your text as you write. Be especially careful with *discrete/discreet*, *principal/principle*, and *dependant/dependent*, as they're often confused with each other.

Many words that are merely similar are often confused, eg territories or waters are not *unchartered* but *uncharted* (namely unmapped). And while the plural of *medium* can technically be *mediums*, you're better off using *media* to avoid suggesting 'group of people who claim to be psychic'.

In every one of these examples the wrongly chosen word is still a valid word in its own right, so a spelling and grammar check may not spot it. If you're unsure whether you've picked the right word, always check it using a reliable dictionary: www.onelook.com is a good place to start.

Confusing a *and* an

The old rule about '*a* before a consonant, *an* before a vowel' refers to a word's *sound* not its spelling – it's why we write *a* university not *an* university. The trick to getting *a/an* right, then, is to trust your ears not your eyes:

✗ *A* HTML server *[you'd never say 'a aitch']*
✓ *An* HTML server

Confusing what *and* which

Getting *what* confused with *which* isn't an egregious mistake, but it can make your writing sound a little off-key. The difference is that you use *what* when referring to something specific and *which* for choices. Hence:

✓ *What*'s that you're drinking?
✓ *Which* one's mine?

Grammatical myths

We've looked at some of the most common grammatical errors. Now let's look at some grammatical myths and areas where you have some flexibility in the rules.

The first point to consider is that English is a living language, so what used to be considered wrong may no longer be so; history's littered with stories of outrage at some grammatical infraction that became the norm. There have always been and always will be battles between prescriptivists (who argue that a language is defined by its rules) and descriptivists (who argue that what counts is how language is actually used). As with much in life, the best approach is to avoid the extremes and apply common sense: grammatical rules should serve clarity, not the other way round.

That said, the principle of 'the customer is always right' applies to readers as well. If you suspect your readers might include misguided pedants who spit with rage and uncap their green pens at any supposed infraction of what *they* consider right, you might be better off avoiding certain constructions even if you know they're OK. This caveat applies especially to that most persistent of grammatical shibboleths, the split infinitive – so let's look at that first.

'Thou shalt not split an infinitive' is a myth, plain and simple. What the myth claims is that it's wrong to insert a word between [to + verb], a famous example being Star Trek's '*To boldly go* where no man has gone before'. In one sense this myth is true in that you can't 'split an infinitive' anyway, since *to* is a preposition (or 'infinitival subordinator', if you want to get even more technical) and not part of the verb form. The myth took root in 1864, with a popular grammar book called *A Plea for the Queen's English* by Henry Alford, a nineteenth-century Latin scholar and Dean of Canterbury. Writers had been blissfully ignoring the myth for centuries before it was invented and grammarians have been debunking it ever since.

As well as being unnecessary, avoiding a split infinitive can also make a sentence clumsy or ambiguous:

✗ It's OK to split boldly infinitives
✓ It's OK to boldly split infinitives

As with 'Thou shalt not split an infinitive', the myth that you can't end a sentence with prepositions (words such as *on*, *with* and *for*) is one that great writers have been ignoring for centuries. The word *preposition* (literally 'pre-position') is unfortunate in hinting that words in this category come before something else; but look up the word in any respectable dictionary and you'll see that prepositions are defined as *usually* coming before the word they relate to. And ha! There you have it: 'relate to', a perfectly respectable example of ending a sentence with a preposition. Yes, you could change the sentence to end with '... the word to which they relate'. But this sort of prissiness, to paraphrase a quote commonly misattributed to Winston Churchill, is the sort of English 'up with which you need not put'.

That said, although it's never wrong to end a sentence with a preposition you may want to avoid doing so if a more important word needs to come at the end for emphasis or stylistic reasons: for example, 'He was best friends with the Army captain, with whom he was killed' sounds more dignified and respectful than 'He was best friends with the Army captain he was killed with'.

Another persistent myth is 'Thou shalt not start sentences with *and* or *but*.' And so Shakespeare, Charles Dickens, Jane Austin, Chaucer, and the authors of the King James Bible were 'wrong', were they? Good writers have been starting sentences with conjunctions (also known as 'coordinators') since at least the tenth century. As the names *conjunction* and *coordinator* suggest, the function of this category of words is to join or coordinate ideas. Supporters of the myth claim that the joining/coordination can only occur within sentences, not between them. But there's no evidence or logic for this belief whatsoever.

Another myth is that it's wrong to write sentence fragments, namely words punctuated as if they form full sentences when they don't. Is it wrong to write them? No. As I've just shown you by writing 'No' followed by a full stop ('period' in US English), it's perfectly fine to write sentence fragments of as little as one word. There is no reason whatsoever to insist that all strings of words ending with a full stop, question mark or exclamation mark need to be complete sentences.

That said, avoid writing 'garden-path' sentence fragments, namely fragments that start out looking like a full sentence and hence give readers linguistic whiplash by slamming to a screeching halt:

✓ Writing sentence fragments? Perfectly fine. Usually.

✗ While it's jarring to read a sentence fragment you expect to be a full sentence that's not.

Also, be tasteful – like spices, properly formed sentence fragments add zing in moderation but can become overpowering if overused. Too many sentence fragments can make your writing sound like adspeak of the form, 'Fresh ingredients. Naturally.'

A slightly more ambiguous area of grammatical mythology is whether you can treat plural nouns as singular, because sometimes you can and sometimes you can't. With some irregular plurals, it's clearly wrong to treat them as singular: *criteria* and *bacteria* are the plural forms of *criterion* and *bacterium*, so constructions such as 'the criteria *is*' and 'the bacteria *was*' are just plain wrong. But what about *data*? It's the plural of *datum*, so is it really OK to write a sentence such as, 'During failover, data *is* transferred from server A to server B'?

Yes, it's fine. Remember uncountable nouns (aka mass nouns), which are always treated as singular? Unless you're actually differentiating between data and *datum* (piece of data), it's now accepted practice to treat the word *data* as either countable (plural) or uncountable (singular) depending on context, and the distinction can be useful. For example, compare these two sentences:

✓ The data on markets and products *are* being gathered
✓ All data *is* transferred between servers

In the first sentence, the fact that there are two types of data is significant, so treating *data* as countable (hence plural) makes sense; but in the second sentence, *data* is being considered as a collective whole, so an uncountable noun (hence singular) is preferable.

Still not convinced? Consider the word *agenda*: it's a Latin plural (the singular form being *agendum*) but an English singular, so you're correct to write 'the agenda *is*'. You could call an agenda item 'an agendum' – but you'd risk sounding extremely pedantic.

And if you think it's a fudge to say 'countable or uncountable, depending on context', consider that there's a significant set of nouns for which this is the case. Take liquids:

✓ I drink coffee / She ordered three coffees
✓ He poured water on the fire / Still waters run deep

Here's another example of a technically plural subject being treated (correctly) as plural or singular, depending on context:

✓ A counterfeiter was arrested yesterday and thousands of pounds *were* found in his wardrobe
✓ £10,000 *was* transferred to your account

The first sentence is implicitly referring to coins or notes (plural); but in the second sentence, '£10,000 were' would sound weird, because what's being implicitly referred to is a sum (singular) of money. Subject-verb agreement based on tacit meaning rather than strict adherence to grammar is so respectable it's even got its own name: synesis or notional agreement, as opposed to formal agreement.

We've just seen how sometimes it's OK to treat plural nouns as singular – is it OK to treat singular nouns as plural? Sometimes, yes. Consider:

✓ The audience stamped *their* feet / One third of crimes *are* not reported

Insist on treating 'audience' or 'third' as singular and your sentences sound absurd:

✗ The audience stamped *its* foot / One third of crimes *is* not reported

That doesn't mean you *must* use the plural. As with the 'thousands of pounds' v '£10,000' distinction given earlier, the point is that you have the choice between plural and singular. Compare these two sentences:

✓ The audience left their seats
✓ The audience *was* splashed in colours from the light show

In the first sentence, *audience* is referring to individuals and hence plural; whereas in the second sentence, it's referring to a unified mass of people, and hence singular. If someone tries to claim you're wrong to treat the word *audience* as a plural, ask *them* whether they'd write 'The police is'. (*They*, and its derivatives, has long been accepted by most authorities as a gender-neutral singular.) Both *police* and *audience* are collective nouns (words indicating a group of people or things) and, as the word *police* proves, sometimes it's not only OK but even necessary to treat singular collective nouns as plural.

If that misguided pedant still tries to insist you're wrong, you can patiently explain that *audience* is both a collective noun and a synecdoche, so while it's syntactically singular it's also semantically plural: a collective noun being one referring to a group of people or things (*orchestra*, *team*, *government*, etc), and synecdoche (pronounced sin-NEK-duh-key) being a figure of speech where a part stands for a whole (eg 'Whitehall' for the UK government) or whole for the parts (eg 'orchestra' for all the players). Synecdoches explain why you can say things such as:

✓ The White House spoke to Whitehall

… without a pedant complaining, 'Buildings can't talk to each other!'

CHECK YOUR SPELLING AND CAPITALISATION

There's not much to say about spelling beyond the importance of deciding which language variant to adopt and sticking to it (eg UK v US spelling), and remembering to run a spelling check: after all, a word's either correctly spelt or it isn't. What does require discussion, as it's both complex and affects meaning, is capitalisation.

Strictly speaking, capitalisation isn't a part of grammar and spelling but of what's called orthography, namely a language's written conventions including capitalisation, spelling, hyphenation and punctuation. That said, outside of linguistics departments most people talk of 'grammar and spelling' rather than 'orthography' and consider a word's capitalisation to be part of its spelling – and since this book's a practical guide rather than an academic treatise, we'll do the same (as does Word's grammar and spelling checker).

First off, why's capitalisation important? You can't hear the difference in spoken English, so why does it matter in written English? Two reasons: first, wrong capitalisation can harm your credibility by making you look illiterate; second (and more importantly), wrong capitalisation can change a word's meaning. For example, 'city' refers to any town deemed important enough for city status, whereas 'the City' can mean only London's Square Mile. Similarly, compare May/may, Apple/apple, and Polish/polish. Collectively, words that change their meaning (and sometimes their pronunciation) depending on whether they're capitalised are known as capitonyms.

The main rule you need to follow is to capitalise only proper nouns, meaning the names of specific things or people (*Microsoft, Tuesday, Fred*) and not common nouns, meaning words for something generic or non-specific (*company, day, person*). As a rule of thumb, if you can write an indefinite article (*a* or *an*) in front of the word, it's functioning as a common noun and hence lowercase: *Queen Elizabeth* (specific queen) but *a queen*; or *Bank of England* (specific bank) but *a bank*. So you write 'I went to the *bank* at lunchtime and saw the *board* members afterwards.'

Most business writing is full of common nouns wrongly capped. In fact, the only example I've ever found in corporate documentation of the opposite occurring – a proper noun wrongly written without an initial cap – is the very esoteric *Student-t copula*, a mathematical function often mentioned in actuarial documentation. It's named not after *student* as in 'person who studies' (which would make it a common noun and hence lowercase) but after the pseudonym used by the statistician William Sealy Gosset, making it a proper noun and hence capped.

Let's look at the most frequent capitalisation problems and how to fix them.

Common nouns in headings

Only in headings is it OK to capitalise common nouns, your choices being:

- Title Case Where You Capitalise all but Small Words
- Sentence case where you capitalise headings like sentences

But even with headings, lowercase is better than caps:

- Title case looks old-fashioned – look at most newspapers and magazines and you'll see that they nearly always use sentence case
- Title case risks ambiguity with capitonyms (Pole/pole, May/may, etc), whereas sentence case doesn't.

Take this heading I saw in *The Times*: 'Tributes to Beloved author Morrison after death at 88' – the fact that 'author' is lowercase helps us see straight away that the story is about the death of Toni Morrison, best known as the author of the novel *Beloved*. If instead 'author' had been capitalised, the headline could easily be misread as being about the death of an author who was beloved.

Common nouns in body text

Never capitalise common nouns in body text, namely text other than headings (and even in headings it's preferable not to, as we've just seen in the previous section).

The following words are commonly capitalised when they shouldn't be:

- In all businesses, *board*, *business unit*, *legal entity*, *function* (as in Risk *Function*) and currencies (*euros*, *pounds*, etc)
- In banking, the names of financial instruments, eg *bond*, *swap* and *FX spot*
- In insurance, *internal model*, *life*, (as in general insurance v *Life*), *normal* (as in *Normal* v *lognormal*), *technical provisions*, *own funds*, and *cat* (as in short for 'catastrophe')

This rule about never capitalising common nouns isn't about pedantry but about clarity. If you write *Megabank's Credit Service* when you merely mean *Megabank's credit service*, you risk fooling readers into believing the bank has an actual product called Credit Service. Similarly, writing catastrophe risk as *CAT risk* (as it's often and inexplicably miswritten) implies a risk associated with C-something, A-something, T-something.

Abbreviations

Just because an abbreviation is capitalised it doesn't mean the underlying words need to be as well (unless they're proper nouns, of course). Hence 'BAU' stands for *business as usual* not *Business as Usual*. Similarly, *probability distribution forecast*, *user acceptance testing*, etc.

What about the abbreviations themselves? Ask yourself if you can pronounce the abbreviation as a word:

- Yes? It's an acronym, meaning you treat it like any other noun: initial cap for proper nouns (eg *Nato*) and all lowercase for common nouns (eg *radar*)
- No? It's an initialism, meaning you cap all the letters (eg *PDF* for 'pee-dee-eff')

By the same logic, the abbreviation for identity is pronounced as 'aye-dee' so it's written as *ID* not *id* (unless you mean the Freudian term as in 'id, ego and superego'). Similarly, *DB* and *IP*. And make sure you cap all the letters not just the first, eg the correct abbreviation for 'request for quote' is *RFQ* not *Rfq* (as I've often seen it miswritten).

Portmanteaus

Portmanteau words are nouns made by blending two nouns, eg motor + hotel = motel. The capitalisation rule for portmanteaus is the same as for abbreviations: lowercase for common nouns and capped for proper nouns only. Hence *brunch* (breakfast + lunch) but also *Chunnel* (Channel Tunnel).

Writing horrors such as *FinTech* (financial technology) instead of *fintech* is as wrong as writing malware as MalWare, workaholic as WorkAholic or smog as SmOg.

Commercial names and terms

Company names are proper names and hence usually capped conventionally: initial cap if spelt out as words (Amazon, Apple, Facebook) or all caps if initialisms (BP, BBC, HSBC). I say 'usually', because many companies and their products use quirky capitalisation, eg PowerPoint, AngularJS, easyJet and PricewaterhouseCoopers (abbreviated to PwC).

If in doubt always check a reliable source, such as the vendor's own website. If you wrote 'Javascript' in a business proposal, picky clients might justifiably wonder, 'If they can't even get "JavaScript" right, how sloppy is their software?'

Also, make sure you write 'plc' (as in 'public limited company') as all lowercase: many style guides (such as the BBC's and the Guardian's) insist on it, as do most companies with 'plc' in their name, eg Aviva plc and HSBC plc.

Job titles

Lowercase, please. Quality publications often don't capitalise even the most important job titles, eg 'the pope' and 'the US president', and capping every occurrence of a job title makes text shrill, ugly and hard to read:

✗ The *Chief Actuary* reports to the *Chief Operating Officer*
✓ The *chief actuary* reports to the *chief operating officer*

An exception is that you do cap a job title if it forms part of a person's name: Queen Elizabeth, Pope Francis, and so on.

Names of teams, departments, etc

Names of companies are capped while job roles aren't (business analyst, banker, technical writer) but what about the middle ground of departments, teams and so on? It's a bit of a grey area: sometimes a cap can be useful for distinguishing a team's name from a common noun, as in 'The report was produced by Finance' – but where there's no ambiguity and the name's effectively a common noun then lowercase is preferable, as in 'The report was produced by the finance department.'

Compound modifiers

Earlier we looked at compound modifiers. To refresh your memory, they're instances of two or more words operating as a unit to modify another word, eg '*man-eating* tiger'. You indicate compound modifiers with hyphens, and you don't cap the words unless they're proper nouns:

✗ *User Interface* module, *End of Year* report
✓ *user-interface* module, *end-of-year* report
✓ *Nato*-controlled zone

To fix ungainly compound modifiers, try abbreviations or flipping the word order:

✗ The group's solvency-capital-requirement calculation
✓ The group's SCR calculation
✓ Calculating the group's solvency capital requirement (or SCR)

Caps (and underlining) for emphasis

Avoid using capitalisation and underlining for emphasis:

- ✗ Capitalising words for emphasis is NOT wise because it CAN make readers mistake the capitals for abbreviations (and it looks childish and amateur)

  WRITING WHOLE SENTENCES IN CAPITALS IS EVEN WORSE. CAPITALISED SENTENCES 'SHOUT' AT READERS AND REDUCE READING SPEED (BY ABOUT 15%) BECAUSE ALL LETTERS ARE THE SAME HEIGHT, LACKING THE CONTOURS OF LOWERCASE LETTERS
- ✗ <u>Similarly, avoid underlining for emphasis. Underlining looks ugly and old-fashioned, can fool people into thinking the text is a hyperlink, and interferes with punctuation and descenders, ie the 'tails' on g, j, p, q, y. Keep underlining for hyperlinks only.</u>

Instead, use bold and italics. But go easy: especially with bold, which is more strident than italics. Readers prefer you to get their attention with a tap on the shoulder rather than a kick on the shin.

Lowercase as a cultural marker

Some people, especially those in creative industries, use lowercase where standard usage is to capitalise. For example, they'll start an email with 'dear' rather than 'Dear', sign off with 'regards' instead of 'Regards' and even write their own name (and yours!) all lowercase.

Some readers feel that unorthodox lowercasing makes writing look hip and cool, gives it a breezy informality. Others (probably the majority) will consider it plain wrong or an affectation.

As with so many aspects of writing, it's a matter of knowing your audience and gauging the context. But if in doubt, play safe and stick to standard capitalisation.

FIX YOUR FORMATTING

At this stage you're concentrating on making your formatting effective and consistent.

Use white space effectively

Scan your pages – do they look either crowded or bitty? If so, consider adjusting paragraph lengths. Remember, though, that what looks like a short paragraph across the full width of a page becomes much longer in a table column or newspaper-column layout (and vice versa). Recall as well the importance of paragraphing for grouping ideas.

Also consider adjusting line spacing, both the spacing of lines within a paragraph and the spacing between paragraphs. If you do adjust line spacing, make sure you do it by adjusting paragraph styles and not by adding extra carriage returns. And if you're working to a standard house style or template, remember that it's best to adhere to it.

Avoid blank lines and double spaces

Use only one carriage return between paragraphs. Any template (eg in Microsoft Word) worth its salt will have paragraph styles with built-in line spacing anyway.

Also, use only a single space after a full stop – using two spaces is an outdated convention from typewriters, which couldn't adjust letter spacing and which had only a single, non-proportional typeface (ie typeface where all the letters are the same width).

Here are a couple of useful tricks if you're using Microsoft Word:

- You can replace multiple carriage returns with single ones, by finding ^p^p and replacing it with ^p. You may need to do more than one round of 'replace all', though. For example, if the text has any triple carriage returns, replacing ^p^p with ^p will replace any triples with doubles – which in turn will become singles in the next round of 'replace all'. Just keep doing successive rounds of 'replace all' till the number of replacements hits zero.
- Similarly, you can replace multiple spaces with single ones, by typing two spaces in the Find field and a single space in the Replace field. Also, Word's grammar and spelling options include an option that prevents double spaces.

Use numbers for sequences and bullets otherwise

Use numbers where the order of items is significant (eg steps in a process, or rankings) and bullets otherwise.

Use colours effectively

If your company has an official colour palette, use it. It's almost certainly been created by a graphic designer who understands your company's branding rules but also more subtle factors such as colour harmony and contrast (eg to help people who are colour blind).

Around 5% to 10% of people have some degree of colour blindness, the most common being red/green, so it's a good idea to find ways other than colour to provide contrast. With a simple Google search you can find websites and information on browser plugins that show you (assuming you're a fully sighted person) how colours degrade for people who are colour blind. Also remember that colour contrasts can be lost if a colour document is printed in greyscale. In particular, always avoid red on black (or vice versa) as they're indistinguishable when printed in greyscale. One way to reduce the risk of colour loss is to replace solid shading with patterned or textured shading – but not where you have text on top, as any form of patterning or texture interferes with text and so reduces legibility.

Avoid colours just for prettiness rather than to highlight something of importance such as groupings or themes. As with graphics added for prettiness rather than meaning, readers will puzzle over the colours' significance or even draw their own, often wrong, inferences.

Finally, consider that you can often exploit the cultural associations of colours, such as red for danger and green for positives ('Go!' in traffic lights, eco-friendliness, etc) – but do remember colour blindness and the fact that red/green confusion is the commonest form. Also bear in mind that colour connotations can be culturally specific. In many Asian countries, white is associated with mourning and funerals. A famous marketing misfire was Ronald McDonald in Japan, his white face being perceived as a death mask.

For more about the subtle effects of colour, particularly online, check out *Webs of Influence – the Psychology of Online Persuasion* by Nathalie Nahai, which also has lots of other insights about psychology as it applies to the web.

Minimise footnotes (or endnotes)

Footnotes (or endnotes) force readers to glance back and forth between the body text and the note, which interrupts their reading and hence their understanding.

It's best to restrict footnotes or endnotes (if you have them at all) to citing sources. If you add supplementary information but only occasionally, your readers will forever be wondering whether it's worth the effort of looking up the note in case they miss something – then feeling dissatisfied whichever choice they make.

Whenever possible, keep supplementary information in the body text rather than burying it in footnotes or endnotes.

Check your margins

Sometimes page elements accidentally push into the margins, or margin settings vary between sections – so it's always worth scanning your margins for any discrepancies.

A good tip is to zoom out enough to fit several pages onto your screen, as this makes discrepancies easier to spot and renders the words illegible so they don't distract you.

Incidentally, deliberately obscuring text to concentrate on design aspects is called 'greeking'. The text used for greeking is often legible but deliberately incomprehensible, the commonest example being the nonsense Latin known as *Lorem Ipsum*.

Check headers and footers

As we saw earlier in the section on Word templates, a good template will have well-designed headers and footers requiring little or no maintenance. That said, it's always worth checking headers and footers for missing page numbers, and for any portrait-width headers/footers in landscape pages (or vice versa) – but if you followed the earlier advice to centre your headers/footers, this won't ever be a problem.

Also (and specifically if you're using Microsoft Word) check for non-continuous page numbering, which can happen if you have section breaks and the numbering for one or more sections is set to 'Start at' rather than 'Continue from previous section'. This problem is one reason that it's wise to minimise (or eliminate) section breaks. For example, in Word you can force each Heading 1 to start on a new page without needing section breaks – to do so, tick **Page break before** in the paragraph style.

Check for awkward page breaks

During early drafts, it's not worth fretting about awkward page breaks because the text is in flux. But once your text is fairly stable, it's worth looking for problems such as table headers decapitated from the rest of the table, and lines of text stranded at the bottom or top of a page: what are called orphans and widows, an orphan being a line of text stranded at a paragraph's start (ie the bottom of a page) and a widow one stranded at the end of a paragraph (ie the top of the following page).

If you're using Microsoft Word, here are some tips for reducing the chance of awkward page breaks:

- To keep a paragraph on the same page as the next one, tick the paragraph property **Keep with next**
- To stop table headings becoming 'decapitated' when the table spreads over more than one page, tick the table property **Repeat as header row**
- To make it easier to scan for awkward page breaks, use the same trick as when checking your margins, namely zooming out till you've several pages on the screen at the same time

(OPTIONAL) ADD A GLOSSARY

If you're creating a document that will be used only within your company, it's best not to create a glossary per document but instead a global glossary (eg on an intranet site) to which all other documentation can point using a URL. That way, you save the maintenance burden of creating dozens of stand-alone glossaries and (worse) the risk that glossaries in different documents contradict each other. The only time it makes sense to create a document-specific glossary is if the document's needed by someone who don't have access to your central glossary, eg a client or a financial regulator.

Irrespective of whether the glossary you're creating is centralised or local, here are some suggestions for making sure it's effective.

Define terms in your body text too

Define your glossary terms in the main body of your document as well as the glossary, so readers don't have to keep flicking back and forth every time they come across an unfamiliar term.

In the body text, you only need to define each term the first time you mention it. It's the same with abbreviations, where the convention is to write the word/phrase in full followed by its abbreviation in parentheses, after which you can use the abbreviation on its own:

> This report explains how we plan to implement our cybersecurity *target operating model (TOM).* All business units will be affected by the *TOM.*

Capitalise terms only if they're proper nouns

Use lowercase for all glossary terms (and index entries) that are common nouns, to distinguish them from proper nouns. This is especially important when the same word changes meaning according to whether it's capped – in which case your glossary should include both, as separate entries:

group	(*lowercase*) Mega Insurance Group and its legal entities, eg 'The group is applying for internal model approval.'
Group	(*uppercase*) Abbreviation for Mega Insurance Group as an entity in its own right, eg 'Group will liaise with the regulator on behalf of all legal entities within the *group*.'

Highlight words that are terms themselves

If a definition contains text that's a glossary term in its own right, it's a good idea to add a highlighted cross-reference, eg *group* in the example above. A good tip if you're using Microsoft Word is to use a heading style (say Heading 6) for your 'glossary term' column (so you can cross-refer to glossary terms) and add a *character* style on top – that way, your cross-references pick up the character style applied to the glossary term so it stands out from the rest of the text.

Avoid preambles

Avoid preambles to your glossary definitions, such as *This refers to*, or even *The* and *A*. Just go straight into the definition, the same way that a dictionary does:

eligible complainant	~~This refers to a~~ Person eligible for having their complaint handled according to UK regulations.

Start with a definition

Make sure your definition actually starts with a definition:

bank asset	~~It's important to ensure that all bank assets are enabled before going live~~. Any of BankX's applications, either internal or third-party.

Keep terms singular

Keep terms singular, as in a dictionary. For example, not this:

apps	Software applications, especially those downloaded onto a mobile device.

… but this:

app	Software application, especially one downloaded onto a mobile device.

Separate definitions from elaborations

For clarity it's best to have each definition in a stand-alone paragraph, with any elaborations in following paragraphs:

off-refer	Status of a currency pair when the public can trade it without having to call a salesperson. Off-refer is the normal status for currency pairs – compare with *on-refer*.

Include jargon and synonyms

As we saw earlier when discussing jargon, people sometimes use different terms for the same concept or the same term for different concepts, and sometimes terms change. A glossary is great tool for avoiding confusion, so if you have two terms for the same thing it's a good idea to list both and explain that they're synonyms:

artefact	Another name for *deliverable*.
deliverable	Anything that needs to be produced as part of a project, be it a physical object (such as a document) or something less tangible (such as a new process).

Define abbreviations

If you include abbreviations, it's usually best to have separate entries for what they abbreviate:

CAT	Abbreviation for *client acceptance testing*.
client acceptance testing	Testing performed before handover to a client. Compare with *user acceptance testing* (*UAT*), which is testing performed by a client after the handover.

On the other hand, if you want a pure glossary of abbreviations, it's best not to muddy the waters by defining anything other than the abbreviations themselves.

(OPTIONAL) CREATE AN INDEX

Some people fear that long documents are hard to read. Not so. The second edition of the Oxford English Dictionary contains 59 million words and it's a cinch to find the entry you want (from over 301,000 of them). What makes information easy to find is not size but structure – and, often, a good index. A well-designed index is a thing of beauty. It makes a long document look complete and stamps it with a hallmark of quality. Readers will sense that any writer who's taken the trouble to write an index has probably put effort into the rest of the document.

It's true that Microsoft Word's Find function makes indexes slightly less crucial than in pre-computing days when all books were hard copies, but consider the following:

- The Find function doesn't work on a printed document
- You can't search for what you don't know is there – an index entry shows readers what they might not realise your document covers, and encourages them to explore and reread
- Intelligent, well-designed index entries can:
    - point to a specific word, or even an idea or theme (which a text-string search wouldn't find)
    - show all pages on which an entry occurs
    - enable readers to search in multiple ways, eg when looking for 'operational risk' in an index, one reader might look under O for 'operational risk' while another might look under R for 'risks, operational'

Microsoft Word has extensive help on how to create an index. And if you do create an index, remember to capitalise an index entry only if it's a proper noun. For example:

Queen Elizabeth I 120–121
queens of England 119–131

PROOFREAD

Any obstacle to understanding is like a scratch or smear on the window between you and your readers. Even tiny ones can leave readers squinting at your meaning through a blurry pane of misunderstanding. At the proofreading stage, your job is to clean and polish your text until that window's transparent – and after these finishing touches, it will sparkle.

Check you've followed the house style

If your company has a house style, it's wise to follow it. Matters of style can be highly subjective, and a good house style helps you to ensure your document is consistent with other people's in matters such as:

- Writing numbers as words or numerals, eg 'Write one to twelve as words, and 13 onwards as numerals'
- Writing *per cent* as two words (UK) or one (US), or using the % symbol instead
- How to write dates, eg 1 January 2021, 1st January 2021, or January 1, 2021

If your company doesn't have a house style, you can always go with one in the public domain, eg:

- For the UK, the style guide of the *Guardian* (www.theguardian.com/guardian-observer-style-guide-a)
- For the United States, the Chicago Manual of Style (www.chicagomanualofstyle.org)

Even if you know your company's style rules, it's easy to slip up occasionally – so at the proofreading stage it's a good idea to check you've been consistent throughout.

Reread and rewrite – after a break

To produce great writing, be prepared to rewrite and re-rewrite – preferably after a break so you can experience your text as a reader does. Read your own material too soon, when the plaster's still wet, and you'll be too self-conscious of the cracks and joins readers are unlikely to notice because they weren't involved in the construction.

Also, the longer you stare at your text the more likely you are to miss your own errors. You might well have had the experience of editing part of a sentence but accidently leaving traces of the old structure, resulting in a new sentence that's ungrammatical or no longer makes sense. Or found yourself looking at something you wrote a while ago, spotting a howler and thinking, how did I miss *that*?!

If you write something on a Friday afternoon (when you may be tired and prone to making errors), edit it on Monday morning. Even a short break can help, such as editing in the morning what you wrote the previous day, or editing after lunch what you wrote in the morning. And the longer you leave it, the more time you're giving your unconscious time to discover startling new ways to convey your message.

Scan for glitches and inconsistencies

Glitches can be very subtle and easy to overlook, and others not worth checking for until the very last moment when the content's stable: things such as instructions where some steps don't begin with a verb.

A couple of tricks for spotting glitches:

- As well as reading in the normal direction of left-to-right then next line, scan the text vertically. Doing so defamiliarises the text and helps you spot clumsy repetitions (eg consecutive paragraphs starting with the same word) and inconsistencies in lists, tables and instructions (eg a step in an instruction that doesn't start with a verb when all the others do).

- Print your document, or select a bigger zoom than normal (eg 150% if your normal zoom is 100%). Glitches easily overlooked on screen at a normal zoom often leap off a page that's printed or at a larger zoom, such as varying line thicknesses and curly v straight quotes.

Read everything one last time

Edits often introduce new errors, not just in what you've changed but also in what you *haven't* changed. How can this be? Well, changing part of a sentence often knocks it out of whack with the rest. Take this sentence:

> Lots of people, including me, have found it's easy to introduce new errors into their text when they edit

You think that 'Lots of people, including me' is long-winded and decide to trim it to 'I':

> ~~*Lots of people, including me,*~~ *I* have found it's easy to introduce new errors into their text when they edit

That's OK, isn't it? 'I have found it's easy' is perfectly grammatical so there's no need to check the whole sentence, is there? Wrong, because you've missed *their* and *they* that need changing now your sentence's subject has gone from plural to singular:

✗ I have found it's easy to introduce new errors into *their* text when *they* edit

The time to stop proofreading is when you've read *everything*, and *nothing* needs changing.

Run a grammar and spelling check

If you're using Microsoft Word, it's a good idea to use the spelling and grammar checker – but take care not to blithely accept all its recommendations as Word often flags non-errors and misses genuine errors. Also, if Word flags a misspelling and you disagree, check you're actually right before asking Word to learn the word (after which Word won't flag it again).

It's worth considering buying software offering more sophisticated style/grammar capability than Microsoft Word's, such as StyleWriter,

WhiteSmoke, ProWritingAid or Grammarly. They're still fallible and you'll still have to exercise judgement, but they do catch more errors and provide more information.

Some of these tools use a freemium model. For example, you can use Grammarly for free to check your emails and social media postings, but need to pay for full integration with MS-Office applications. You can, however, usually trial premium versions before paying for them. One restriction with such tools is that often they integrate with MS-Office on Windows but not Apple Mac. Your best option is to research what's available, what it costs (if anything), and whether it's got all the features you want.

Check for signs of a draft

Check for any signs that the document is incomplete, typically (in Microsoft Word documents):

- Comments
- Tracked changes
- The word 'draft' in headers, footers, watermarks or the filename
- Occurrences of the text 'ERROR! BOOKMARK NOT DEFINED', indicating a broken or outdated cross-reference (often found in tables of contents). Normally you can fix this problem by updating all fields (see below) – if that doesn't work for a specific cross-reference, you'll just have to redo the cross-reference.

Remember to update all fields

If you're using Microsoft Word, remember to update all fields (table of contents, cross-references, dates, etc). To do so, select all text (Ctrl+A for PCs or Cmd+A for Apple Macs) then right-click and select **Update Field** from the popup menu. If your headers/footers contain fields, you'll have to click inside the header/footer areas to update them separately as, annoyingly, Word won't refresh them otherwise.

(RECOMMENDED) GET REVIEWS

Even if a review is not mandatory (eg for formal sign-off) it's useful for ensuring that your document is factually accurate, complete, properly understood by the target audience, and free from glitches.

For instance, what does the text in the following triangle say?

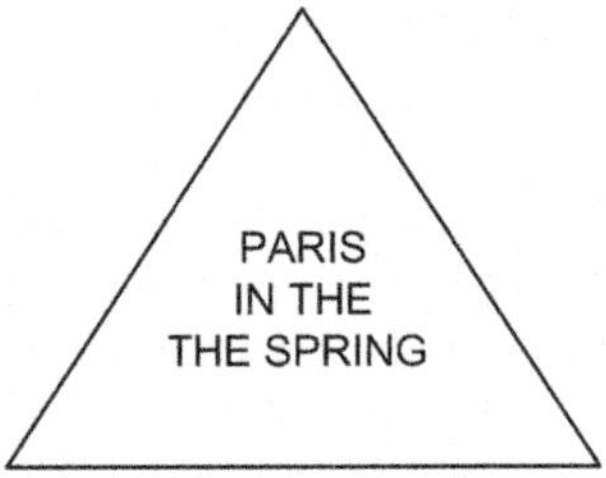

Figure 1.6 Seeing what you expect to see

You think it says 'Paris in the spring'? Read it again. Did you notice 'the the' this time?

The problem with reviewing your own material is that you see what you *expect* to see. As the journalist and presidential speechwriter William Safire once humorously wrote, 'Proofread carefully to see if you any words out.' (Incidentally, these rule-of-language statements that deliberately break their own advice for comic effect are called 'fumblerules'. Look them up, because they make a great checklist of errors to check for.)

So it's always important to get someone else to proofread your text for you. Even professional editors do this. Here are some tips on how to do it.

Working with reviewers

When working with reviewers:

- Avoid giving your reviewers vague requests such as 'Is this OK?' Such requests sound as if you're asking for a pat on the back rather honest criticism.
- Tell each reviewer exactly what to check and what to ignore (eg you need peers to check for accuracy and completeness, not to bicker over your writing style).
- Accept comments graciously: a criticism of your writing isn't a criticism of you.
- Heed reviewers if they say that something's off but can't explain why, because a little digging may uncover gold. Similarly, if someone 'corrects' something that wasn't wrong, their comment still has value because it could indicate your explanation needs work.
- Recognise that some comments will be subjective, even conflicting. The best course is neither to ignore them (they may have a point) nor to try to please everybody (impossible!) but to weigh each opinion and find the balance you consider best.
- If multiple reviewers are involved, discuss the document with everyone at the same time, be it in person or via video conferencing.

You'll save a lot of toing and froing by doing so. And it's best to update the document there and then rather than taking notes, as note-taking can introduce inefficiencies such as comments being overlooked or misinterpreted, or raising further issues that could have been dealt with at the time.

Best order for reviews

It's a good idea to first get reviews from those who best understand the material (to catch factual errors and so on) then move outwards to people increasingly distanced from the topic (for comprehension). Something like this:

1 Yourself, to catch any obviously avoidable errors such as typos. As I mentioned earlier, the time to stop proofreading is when you've read *everything*, and *nothing* needs changing.
2 Peer, to check for accuracy and completeness. Someone from your own team is best placed for understanding, and hence checking, the technical and business complexities.
3 Non-specialist, to check for comprehension. The real test of whether your document works is if an outsider can fully understand and use it, eg successfully complete tasks. In fact, for instructions it's often an excellent idea to observe someone following them, and asking the person to say out loud anything they don't understand.

   Choose a person who's new to the topics you're describing and who knows as much as, or less than, your average intended reader: for example, a person in your company but from a different team; or a technical writer or editor, as they can do a quality check at the same time (see next step).
4 Technical writer or editor, to check that your document's well structured, grammatically correct, concise, properly formatted, and more. These checks can be combined with the comprehension check (see previous step).
5 Normal sign-off channels, for official approval.

Marking up documents for review

If you've asked reviewers to provide comments individually, ask them to add their comments within the document itself rather than, say, in an email response or spreadsheet. If comments are physically separated from the context to which they apply, you'll invariably run into problems such as:

- Page numbers and the text itself changing between drafts, meaning it's often hard or impossible to match comments with the text they refer to

- Comments getting overlooked or forgotten
- Lots of 'noise' caused by reviewers contradicting each other

Incidentally, all of the above problems are why it's better for reviewers to discuss the document as a team rather than individually.

If you're using Microsoft Word, it's worth exploring the review tools available under **File > Options > Proofing**.

For example, **Show readability statistics** gives you readability scores for your document every time you use the grammar and spelling function. These statistics include a Flesch Reading Ease score, calculated using the number of words per sentence and syllables per word: the higher the score, the less complex the text. Word also calculates the Flesch-Kincaid Grade Level score, which rates text by US school grade level, eg a score of 8.0 means it's suitable for an average eighth grader.

Such scoring methods are only rough guides to readability because so many other factors affect comprehension, such as syntax, word choice and continuity of ideas. But these stats do have one big advantage: they're objective. If you're given a document that's a stinker, it's more precise (and tactful!) to ask the person to 'aim for a Flesch–Kincaid score of 8.0' than to say to them, 'Could you make your text less verbose?'

2

MANAGING KNOWLEDGE

In the previous chapter we discovered how best to write a document. But this is only part of the story. At heart, what's important is not creating documents per se but imparting knowledge, a distinction with profound implications:

- Documents are only one vehicle for transferring knowledge, others being wikis, chat-rooms, conference calls, training videos, training courses, chats around the coffee machine (good for picking up stuff you didn't know you didn't know) or even chats in the pub (*in vino veritas*).
- Documenting knowledge is not just about creating well-written content but also about ensuring that it's managed effectively, eg logically organised and regularly updated.
- The word 'knowledge' reminds us that information is inert until it's understood. It's possible to go a step further, from information to knowledge to wisdom, because if knowledge is 'information that is understood' then wisdom is 'knowledge applied wisely'.
- Good knowledge management is not about amassing information; many companies are drowning in information but suffering a drought of knowledge. What it's about is enabling the right people to get the right knowledge at the right times.

In this chapter, we'll explore how best to achieve this goal of 'right people, right knowledge, right times'.

ORGANISE ACROSS EVERYTHING

In a well-structured document, each chapter relates logically to the other chapters. Similarly, in a well-structured *set* of documents, each document relates logically to each of the others in the set. In fact, all the techniques we explored earlier for structuring a single document often work equally well *across* documents, so let's revisit those techniques with that in mind.

Use organisational principles

You can organise entire information repositories (eg SharePoint and wikis) along the lines of 'generic to specific', 'familiar to unfamiliar', 'chronological', eg:

External > Clients > Projects
Internal > Business Units > Functions

One risk of organising information by business function or department is that it can create 'us and them' barriers – if it's feasible, consider organising by workflows instead. For example, if you're an agile software company, rather than dividing first by team then by user stories, consider dividing first by user stories then by function.

Another common consideration, especially on a large change programme, is keeping project-related documentation separate from deliverables. Why? Because what typically happens when the project gets wrapped up is that the project documentation needs to be archived: and that's a lot easier to do if it's clearly segregated rather than mixed in with the documents needed for business as usual.

Work top-down

Just as with a document you determine your chapters (Heading 1s) then your major chapter divisions (Heading 2s) and so on, so too you can look across all knowledge (for your project, office or even entire company) to find the big themes then divide content that way. For example, suppose you're a software company working on multiple projects where coding conventions, tools and methods are pretty universal. You could structure by project, like this:

- Project A (coding conventions, tools, methods)
- Project B (coding conventions, tools, methods)

But this structure obscures the fact that the coding conventions, tools and methods *across* projects are largely universal. So a better structure would be:

- Coding conventions (standard, project-specific)
- Tools (standard, project-specific)
- Methods (standard, project-specific)

Essentially, this approach is the same principle as choosing columns and rows for tables: first, slice everything by whatever you want to emphasise (equivalent to a table's columns) then dice by whatever's secondary (equivalent to a table's rows).

Use unique names

The principle of making each document heading unique is easy to transpose to the meta-level: just make the name of every document library (or wiki space, Google Drive folder, etc) unique as well.

CREATE A UNIVERSAL TAXONOMY

Just as you can apply a standard taxonomy (naming and classification scheme) to documents, so too you can apply one to all your document libraries, intranet sites and so on. As with filenames, it's a good idea to use standard elements arranged from generic to specific.

SHORTEN THE READER'S JOURNEY

Always remember that the fundamental goal of managing knowledge is to transfer understanding between people's heads. According to what's known as the principle of least effort, people seek information using the easiest means available – *and stop looking once they've found minimally acceptable results*. This means that enabling people to find the wrong (eg outdated) information before the right information can be more dangerous than preventing them from finding it at all.

Let's look at some effective ways to shorten the reader's journey.

Create a single entry point

You know those board maps you sometimes get outside stations and in touristy villages, the ones with a big dot or arrow saying 'You are here'? Your information repository needs the same thing, a home page with clear paths that readers can follow to find whatever information they need. It also helps to avoid information getting siloed per project, department, or whatever – an important point we'll look at soon in more depth.

Choose flexible searching over rigid hierarchies

Avoid folder hierarchies, as they force readers to burrow deep to find the information they want and give them only one path to finding information. Instead, use the native search/filter/group/sort capabilities of your information repository to enable readers to find information according to their own, often highly subjective, search criteria.

Keep information within reach

Keep information as close as possible to wherever your readers are most likely to need it (or see it). Let's call this the 'fingertips principle', ie always striving to put knowledge as close as possible to the reader's fingertips.

For example, if you're documenting software, create online help instead of separate user guides; or put software installation instructions in a readme file. Similarly, make policies (or at least their URLs) visible from where their target audience is most likely to see them. For instance, even if Human Resources stores all company policies, you'd be wise to add the risk policy's URL to the risk department's home page rather than relying on risk managers knowing they have to visit HR's home page.

COLLABORATE

Have you ever told yourself, 'I have to hide this information because it's a draft, and I don't want people thinking it's finished'? This is counterproductive thinking. Why?

- ✗ Your fear of misunderstandings is unfounded – all you have to do is add the word 'draft'
- ✗ You're hogging information others may be able to complete, and holding up everyone else in the dependency chain for that information
- ✗ You're risking Chinese whispers – you don't know the answer to A, so you ask person B who asks person C, who's not really sure but suggests you look at document D – which is out of date, but the only person who knows that is person E.

One of the great advantages of wikis (and, to a lesser extent, document management systems such as SharePoint), is that content is available to everyone. Consequently:

- ✓ Everyone who knows the answers can see what needs fixing, and is motivated to do so
- ✓ Readers can offer instant feedback – including clients!
- ✓ Dependency chains are eliminated
- ✓ Drafts are easier to manage

SHARE KNOWLEDGE ACROSS PROJECTS

A lot of firms have content-management systems but their contents (or even the CMSs themselves) are often siloed per project, business unit, or whatever. This means that a lot of valuable knowledge that could benefit another team isn't shared, so the firm is forever reinventing the wheel to solve common problems. For this reason, it's a great idea to have a company-wide knowledge base for any knowledge that applies universally.

Some information may need to be kept confidential to a subset of people: but if you structure your knowledge base well, and permission it correctly, you can gain the benefits of sharing knowledge without causing confidentiality problems.

NURTURE INFORMATION

Knowledge bases are like gardens: without regular pruning, weeding, planting and feeding they turn into either a barren dustbowl or a sprawling, overgrown mess. Here are some techniques for encouraging people to keep your knowledge crop well-tended:

- ✓ To encourage regular site visits, provide informational 'food' to encourage foraging, eg: regular news items; material exclusive to the site you want people to visit ('new starter' material being a great way to encourage visits from day one); and fun material, photos, etc, to make the site enjoyable to visit and to open people's imaginations to the site's possibilities.
- ✓ To encourage people to contribute new content, provide 'seed' material such as headings and partial descriptions.
- ✓ To help keep content fresh, use native content-management tools such as a wiki plug-in that flags pages not updated for a specified period.
- ✓ To wean people off emails and onto knowledge bases, start conversation threads on the knowledge base rather than in emails.

AVOID DUPLICATION

The software development principle of don't repeat yourself (DRY) applies equally to documentation. Let's look at some common duplication issues and how you can avoid them:

- ✗ Versioning by filename (document_v1, etc)

  Use the native versioning of whatever tool you're using. Wikis, SharePoint, Google Drive – they all automatically capture the version history of a page/document, making it unnecessary to save the same content under different names simply to keep a record of earlier drafts.
- ✗ Copying and pasting a chunk of text from one place to another

Replace the duplication with a URL or cross-reference. For example, rather than repeating what you've written elsewhere in a document, simply write: 'For more information, see <URL/cross-ref>'. Here, organisational principles such as 'generic to specific' can be enormously powerful, eg:

This client installation is the same as the generic installation described in <URL/cross-reference>, except that ...

Another solution is to insert the duplicated content as a shared/reused component, so that when the original is updated the duplicate is as well. Content reuse is the essence of single-sourcing tools (such as MadCap Flare and Author-it), but also possible in some content-management tools (such as the wiki tool Confluence) and even Microsoft Word (using bookmarks).

✗ 'Hand-typing' content that could be automated

Use any auto-generation tools available. Such tools are especially useful for documentation that is largely data-based rather than narrative-based, eg status reports can often be auto-generated by project-management software.

✗ Maintaining the same content across different repositories

Combine the contents into a single source. If different repositories are being used because the audiences differ, consider either changing the user permissions so all audiences can use the same site; or create a repository for information that's common across the company.

✗ Maintaining content that is publicly available, eg standard IT concepts or descriptions of third-party products

Replace your text (or uploaded content) with a URL to a public source such as Wikipedia and vendor websites, ie follow the 'outsourcing principle' we explored earlier.

DESIGN FOR OBVIOUSNESS

In an influential book called *The Design of Everyday Things*, author Donald Norman introduced the notion of 'affordance', an example being a handle on the pull side of a door and a plate on the push side since the handle affords pulling and the plate affords pushing. And isn't it frustrating to encounter doors where the push side has a handle? Or a written instruction 'Push'? Any door that needs written instructions has failed, because the design should make its usage obvious. (I've seen doors that say 'Automatic door. Press button here to open' – a spectacular failure of design and documentation.)

Ask yourself whether you can make your products, services and internal processes so obvious that they require little or no documentation. For example:

- Can you make company procedures more obvious, eg through 'funnelling' users such that their initial choices result in an increasingly restricted set of options the further they progress?
- If you're a software company and having to write installation guides, can installations be fully automated, or at least be made so simple that all a user has to do is click a download button then click through a simple series of installation options?

PULL RATHER THAN PUSH

There are two fundamental ways in which to share information:

- Store the information centrally so people can get it when they need it ('pull' model)
- Send the information out, eg by emailing attachments ('push' model)

The 'push' model has many disadvantages:

✗ No control over who gets the information, because any email recipient can forward it

✗ No control over what's done with the information, eg people can modify 'their' version, leading to multiple versions of the truth

✗ If the information changes at source, the email recipient has no way of knowing

✗ The lack of control over who's accessing, modifying and distributing your information means a high risk of data breaches, cyber-attacks, and even prosecution (eg if personally identifiable information falls into the wrong hands)

Compare those 'push' disadvantages with the many advantages of a 'pull' model:

✓ As with an online store, people can get what they want, anywhere, anytime: especially good for firms with offices or clients across multiple time zones

✓ No one needs to second-guess anyone else's information needs, because consumers can decide for themselves what's important to them

✓ Readers can provide feedback and otherwise enrich the information, eg by editing or commenting on a wiki page

✓ Your life is simpler as well as the reader's, because you no longer have to keep informing others of what you've updated and when

✓ You have far more control over who accesses information, drastically reducing the risk of data breaches, cyber-attacks and prosecution for privacy violations

Be aware that any central storage system needs discipline: just chucking a load of documents in shared folders like clothes on the floor of a messy teenager's bedroom will cause you nearly as much pain as a 'push' approach. For this reason, even if you're a small firm it's worth investing in a content-management system (CMS).

Let's look now at how to choose a CMS.

CHOOSE THE RIGHT CONTENT-MANAGEMENT SYSTEM

We've just seen that when going for 'pull' over 'push' you're best off investing in a content-management system (CMS). But what's your best choice?

Most firms run their systems on Microsoft Enterprise, meaning they have SharePoint and Office 365 by default and don't consider anything else. But in my experience, it's best to dispense with all the complexities of documents in a structured environment (SharePoint) and go straight for a wiki such as Confluence, which offers the Wikipedia-style simplicity of directly editable web pages. Yes, SharePoint claims to have wiki capability, but I've found that a SharePoint wiki lacks the intuitiveness and features of a thoroughbred wiki system, and lots of – ahem – 'quirks'.

Also, thoroughbred wikis are better than SharePoint at handling content with many-to-many relationships between chunks of information: it's far easier (for writers and readers alike) to click a URL and go straight to another web page rather than having to click a URL to another document in a SharePoint library, open the document, then search that document's contents.

That said, if your material is mainly text but riddled with interdependencies, it's often a red flag that the structure needs simplifying. One example I encountered was a firm that instead of having a one-to-one relationship between each policy ('*what* to do') and associated instructions ('*how* to do it') had a labyrinthine mix of single policies supported by multiple instruction sets and multiple policies supported by single instruction sets, further complicated by each instruction set referring to other instruction sets. Since there were 65 instruction sets, that's an eye-watering 2,080 possible combinations between the instruction sets alone. (For the mathematically curious, the formula for 'possible combinations between objects' is $n(n - 1)/2$ which, for 65 objects, is $65{\star}64/2 = 2{,}080$.)

RUN A KNOWLEDGE 'HEALTH CHECK'

As proven by natural selection (and agile and lean methodologies, for that matter), dramatic progress can evolve through incremental but continuous enhancements: a slightly better document leads to slightly better cross-team understanding, which leads to a slightly better process, which leads to a virtuous circle of ever-improving operational efficiency. And so on.

But to make a giant leap of progress, consider running a 'health check' across all your firm's documentation to establish what needs fixing. If you do so, it's worth asking all your staff (and potentially clients as well) what they think, perhaps using a web tool such as www.surveymonkey.com or www.smartsurvey.co.uk or a wiki survey plugin.

Good question choices include those we looked at earlier for understanding your readers and gathering your materials. Other good questions include those used in standard SWOT (strengths, weaknesses, opportunities and threats) and gap analyses, such as:

- What knowledge do you (or your team) need?
- What gaps exist in your (or your team's) knowledge?
- What knowledge do you (or your team) need to provide to others?
- What dependencies affect the knowledge you produce and/or consume, eg are you unable to produce report X until team Y has given you Z information?
- Which knowledge-transfer processes could be shortened, and how?
- Which areas are weakest in documentation, and why?
- What have been our most costly knowledge failures, and why? For example, lost sales opportunities, delays in implementation, avoidable bugs, or regulatory fines.

PROVIDE 'KNOWLEDGE ABOUT THE KNOWLEDGE'

You may be familiar with the concept of key-person risk, the idea that if too much knowledge about a particular business activity is locked away in one person's head and that person leaves, the company's in trouble. Knowledge management itself no exception – so remember to explain in writing things such as main contacts (and who deputises in their absence), house style, writing tips, naming conventions, how to operate your content-management system, sign-off procedures, and so on.

3

FURTHER WRITING TIPS

CHOOSING IMAGES

An effective image can bring your writing to life, while badly chosen images can ruin it, so here are a few quick tips:

✓ Use the highest quality images you can

A low-res image might look OK at a normal zoom but horribly pixelated or blurry if your reader uses a high zoom to view it. And few things shriek 'Amateur!' as loudly as a poor image.

✓ Respect copyright

If you're prepared to pay for high-quality images, you'll find thousands on sites such as Getty Images or Shutterstock; and if you're not prepared to pay, use one of the several sites offering royalty-free images such as Pixabay.

Whatever you decide, don't use other people's images unless they're clearly marked as royalty-free – otherwise it's theft.

✓ Avoid anything cheesy

Clip art, and even good imagery used without imagination, looks amateurish and risks boring your readers or audience to death.

For example, don't be among the 99% who use a graphic of jigsaw pieces to show 'how our teams fit together' or clichéd stock photos such as impossibly beautiful people grinning and pointing at a computer screen. If you want photos of people, a professional headshot of a real member of staff or team photo carries far more credibility and meaning.

As for cartoon puppies, Comic Sans font, or anything cutesy, unless you're producing something such as a school newsletter for under-eights just … don't.

✓ Illuminate, don't duplicate

Imagery and text usually work best together when they complement or contrast each other, not when they say exactly the same thing. Think of your favourite print or TV ads, or at least the ones that most stick in your memory – chances are they use imagery metaphorically rather than literally.

PRINTING DOCUMENTS

Here's what to consider when printing documents.

Avoid printing unless you have to

'Saving paper and toner' is the obvious reason for avoiding printing: but it's not the most important, which is that the moment you print a document the information begins to die. Think about it: the moment someone updates the soft copy, your hard copy goes out of date and you have no way of knowing it's happened. Imagine a printed document as a rose cut from its stem: before the paper yellows the information's already wilting. (For this reason, it's wise always to include in your documents a URL to where readers can find the latest online version.) In short, it's wise to print only when any of the following applies:

- ✓ You're happy to have a snapshot of short-lived information such as a project status report for today's meeting (but then again, it may be easier simply to take your laptop into the meeting); or a draft for editing, eg because you find it easier to spot errors on paper than on screen.
- ✓ You need to read the document when you can't get online or don't have your laptop.
- ✓ You're confident that the information is highly unlikely to change during the period you intend to keep the paper copy.

Printer-driver settings

It's worth familiarising yourself with your printer-driver's settings, because they can be extremely useful. Let's explore a few of the most common.

First, most office printers default to double-sided printing rather than single-sided. Usually this is what you'll want anyway, because it halves your paper usage – and note that you can halve your paper usage again with the setting 'two pages to a page'. A standard A4 page shrunk to 50% of its normal size normally remains quite legible. Another reason to print double-sided is to preserve the layout of recto-verso documents, namely documents whose left and right pages mirror each other (most commonly, to keep page numbers on the outer edge of a page). On the other hand, single-sided printing can be helpful if you need to see all pages at once without having to flip pages back and forth to see what's on the reverse side. But, again, even with single-sided printing you can save paper by using the 'two pages to a page' setting.

Second, most colour printers will default to colour. But unless you absolutely must have a document in colour, it's a good idea to override the default and select greyscale instead. Why? Because colour toner's expensive and runs out quickly. Plus if it's a printer with just the one colour cartridge rather than separate cartridges for cyan (blue), magenta (red) and yellow, you have to replace the entire colour cartridge even if only one colour's run out. This can happen really quickly, eg if people are regularly printing slideshows and the company's branding has one dominant colour.

Third, another setting that's increasingly common on company printers is the requirement to enter a password on the printer itself, or tap your security badge on the printer, before you can print your document. Even if a password setting isn't imposed on you by the company's IT department, it's a good one to choose: especially when you need to print a confidential document but the printer's far away, and you want to avoid a mad dash across the office to retrieve your document before anyone else sees it.

Getting fields auto-updated before printing

If you're using Word, you can get fields to auto-update when the document's printed by going to the printing options and ticking **Update fields before printing** and **Update linked data before printing**.

CREATING SLIDESHOWS

This is a book about writing, not giving presentations. But as slides do contain words, it's worth talking about that aspect of using PowerPoint. It's a short talk, because it all comes down to three principles:

- PowerPoint's for slideshows, not documents
- The fewer the words, the better the slides
- Images and animations require taste and restraint

PowerPoint for slideshows, Word for documents

PowerPoint is for creating slideshows, not documents. Its strengths are in *animating* text: it's extremely poor at formatting and paginating text, particularly at high volume. The worst (all too common) mistake is creating slideshows too crowded to be a visual aid for a speaker, but too sparse and starved of context to work as a document.

The only justification for using PowerPoint for documents is if you're giving attendees a hard copy of a presentation they've attended. To see why, let's look at PowerPoint's strengths and weaknesses:

✓ Can animate text
✓ Can include audio and video
✓ Saves duplication if people attending a presentation want a hard copy
✗ Very limited in its formatting and paginating capability, and increasingly impractical the longer the document
For example, you can't insert tables of contents, you can't get text to flow from page to page, and styles are extremely basic. Even Microsoft itself tacitly recognises this problem, because if you select PowerPoint's **Export > Create Handouts**, what does it export to? Microsoft Word

Now let's look at Microsoft Word's strengths and weaknesses:

✓ Far stronger formatting and pagination capability
For example, you can create flexible styles, produce elegant and sophisticated tables, and any text you add automatically creates new pages for text to flow into
✓ Overall, much richer in features
For example, you can create tables of contents, insert cross-references, move sections around much more easily, and more
✓ Better than PowerPoint at producing documents where text predominates
✗ Can't animate text, or use audio and video

In summary:

✓ PowerPoint for slideshows and (if you must) presentation handouts
✓ Word for all other types of document, including briefings and presentation packs of any significant length (say, ten pages or more)

Fewer words means better slides

If you're doing a presentation, the best slideshow is often no slideshow or at most one with imagery only and text as a last resort. If people see text they'll read it, which forces them to stop listening – and an *audience* ('audio' is Latin for 'I listen') is meant to listen. Slideshow text is like subtitles in a film: unless you have hearing difficulties or don't know the language, every word written on the screen is nothing but an annoying distraction.

And on the subject of film, Alfred Hitchcock once made a comment along the lines of, 'First we write the screenplay, then we put the dialogue in,' his point being that film is about telling stories with pictures. If a scriptwriter can replace a line of dialogue with an instruction to an actor they will; why have a character say, 'I don't understand what you mean' when instead you can simply instruct the actor to look confused?

Consider slideshow text like Hitchcock considered dialogue, a last resort. Remember: you need your audience to be listening, not reading.

And whatever you do, never use a slideshow as an autocue. Forcing an audience to hear words they've just read for themselves will bore them, and turning your back on them to read the screen will only disengage them further.

Bad v good slideshows

- Good slides minimise text, sticking to one main point rather than cramming in loads of irrelevant detail. For example:

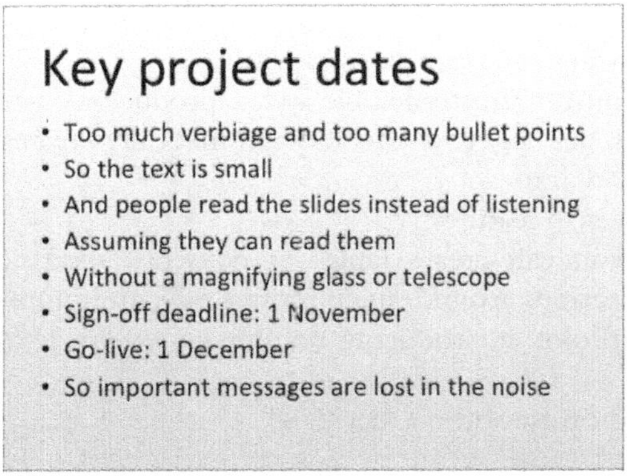

Figure 3.1 Bad slide (too much text and hard to read)

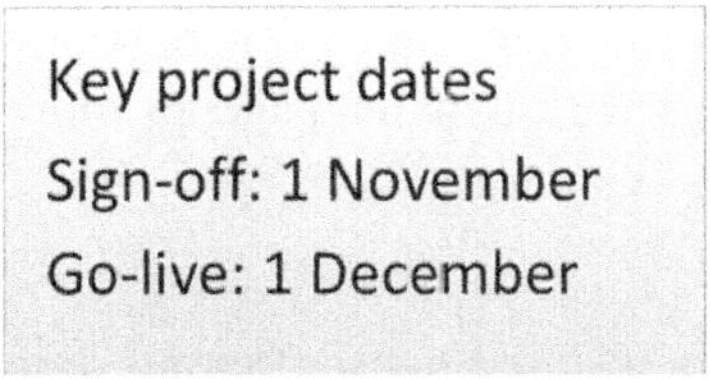

Figure 3.2 Good slide (minimal text and easier to read)

- Good slides use imagery with taste, subtlety and imagination – and perhaps humour. Avoid clichéd clipart, garish colours, data overload, chaotic layouts and meaningless gimmicks. Opt instead for one aesthetically pleasing image and minimal text.
- Good slides use animations with restraint, rather than to swirl and spin viewers towards nausea like a fairground ride.

CREATING PDFs

Saving a document as a PDF (portable document format) fossilises the document's contents, so unless the content is never going to change there's rarely any point in doing so. The only sensible reasons for creating a PDF are as follows:

- ✓ Lock formatting: The formatting of a PDF always remains the same, preventing Word formatting mishaps such as substituted fonts or missing special characters.
- ✓ Lock editing: It's harder for other people to edit PDFs, making information more secure (useful for signed-off documents).
- ✓ Hide sensitive information: Creating a PDF reduces the risk of accidentally exposing sensitive information, such as that found in Word's Properties (author, company, etc).
- ✓ Shrink the file size: PDFs are more compact than Word documents, so saving to PDF can be useful if you're emailing people when file size is a problem. That said, remember that it's usually far better to store documents centrally and email the link instead; the only sensible reason not to do so is if the recipient can't access your document repositories, eg if they are a prospective client or job candidate.
- ✓ Obtain e-signatures: The better PDF creators let you add an e-signature to a document, which can be helpful if documents need to be signed off.

FREE WRITING TOOLS AVAILABLE ON THE WEB

Lots of incredibly useful writing tools are available online. Here are some of my favourites and they're all free.

Writing advice

The Plain English Campaign's website (www.plainenglish.co.uk) has all sorts of useful advice and reference materials, including:

- Short guides to all sorts of writing needs, from how to write in plain English, to proofreading, to writing reports and business emails
- Glossary of legalese – useful both for non-lawyers wanting to understand baffling terms, and to lawyers wanting to replace those baffling terms with ones the public can understand

Another good writing guide is this nifty 16-page booklet from the European Commission:
www.tinyurl.com/EU-HowToWriteClearly

Grammar guides

If you're unsure of any point of grammar, you have many websites to choose from. A particularly good one is www.grammar-monster.com, which even has hundreds of interactive tests.

Dictionaries

OneLook (www.onelook.com) has to be the coolest dictionary on the web, giving you:

- A meta-dictionary (dictionary of dictionaries), so you can find definitions from multiple sources with one hit: including British dictionaries such as Collins, and American dictionaries such as Merriam-Webster
- A reverse dictionary, ie a dictionary for finding a word from its concept. For example, you can search for 'camel with one hump' to find 'dromedary'

Thesauri

A good thesaurus can help you replace tired, grey words with fresh, colourful ones – but avoid using a thesaurus to find pretentious alternatives to simple words.

Thesaurus.com (www.thesaurus.com) gives both synonyms (words with the same meaning) and antonyms (opposite words), plus other goodies that will appeal to word lovers.

Text analysers

Check your text for readability, plagiarism, and search-engine optimisation (SEO), with www.checktext.org.

Fact-checking

To check if something's true or just fake news or an urban myth, a reliable and comprehensive site is Snopes (www.snopes.com).

And for checking who actually said or wrote a famous quote, it's hard to beat Quote Investigator (www.quoteinvestigator.com).

Screenshot software

Both Windows and MacOS provide screenshot tools. They're fairly basic, though, so you may want a third-party app.

My favourite is Gadwin PrintScreen (www.gadwin.com/download). It's only available for Windows not Mac, but even in the freeware version it includes features such include/exclude the screen cursor, and drop shadows for a 'raised off the page' effect.

Touch-typing training

Improve your touch-typing for free, at www.typingstudy.com.

FINAL THOUGHTS

One of my favourite inspirational quotes is from the American cycling legend Greg LeMond who said of cycling, 'It never gets easier, you just go faster.'

Writing's a bit like that, in that you can learn all the rules and put the effort in and it *still* feels hard. But you will be writing better, I promise. I've been in this game for over 30 years and I'm still learning, still occasionally wondering if I'm any good. But when I turn back to see how far I've come, when I blow the dust off my writing samples from years or even months ago, I can feel the difference. You will too.

Here's another pertinent quote. Actually, it's an old joke and it goes like this. A visitor to New York stops a passer-by to ask, 'How do you get to Carnegie Hall?' To which the passer-by replies, 'Practise, practise, practise!'

And that's the main way you get better at writing: 'Write, write, write!' then 'Edit, edit, edit!' To which we can add, 'Read, read, read!' because along with actually putting pen to paper (or fingers to keyboard) the best way to elevate your writing is to read great writers, be they business writers, journalists, novelists, screenwriters, poets, speechwriters, science writers or anyone else whose writing speaks to you. Learn to read at two levels, reader and writer, peering under the skin of sentences to examine how and why they work. And read outside your comfort zone too: if you usually read only newspapers and nonfiction, try some poetry or a novel. You might be amazed at how doing so opens up your imagination and inspires you.

Good luck and keep on writing. And if you've any success stories you'd like to share with me, if you've enjoyed this book, if you want to learn more, I'd love to hear from you.

Julian Maynard-Smith
www.linkedin.com/in/julianms
www.betterbusinesswriting.info

BIBLIOGRAPHY

The following bibliography lists not only books and articles mentioned in the text but also other books that can help you enrich your writing.

Atwood, Margaret (2000) *The Blind Assassin*. Virago.

Bagnall, Nicholas (1993) *Newspaper Language*. Focal Press.

Cowan, Nelson (2010) *The Magical Mystery Four: How is Working Memory Capacity Limited, and Why?* https://www.ncbi.nlm.nih.gov/pmc/articles/PMC2864034/ (accessed 2 November 2020).

Cron, Lisa (2012) *Wired for Story*. Ten Speed Press.

Cutts, Martin (2020) *Oxford Guide to Plain English*. Oxford University Press.

Douglas, Yellowlees (2015) *The Reader's Brain: How Neuroscience Can Make You a Better Writer*. Cambridge University Press.

Epley, Nicholas (2015) *Mindwise*. Penguin Random House.

Fisher, Roger; Ury, William (2011) *Getting to Yes – Negotiating an Agreement without Giving In*. Baker and Taylor.

Geary, James (2012) *I Is an Other: The Secret Life of Metaphor and How It Shapes the Way We See the World*. Harper Perennial.

Goleman, Daniel (2014) *Focus*. Bloomsbury Paperbacks.

Gowers, Ernest; Gowers, Rebecca (2015) *Plain Words*. Penguin Random House.

Hood, Bruce (2013) *The Self Illusion*. Constable.

Jarrett, Caroline; Gaffney, Gerry (2008) *Forms that Work: Designing Web Forms for Usability*. Morgan Kaufmann.

Lakoff, George; Johnson, Mark (2003) *Metaphors We Live By*. University of Chicago Press.

Larkin, Philip (2003) *Collected Poems*. Faber & Faber.

Leith, Sam (2018) *Write to the Point*. Profile Books.

McGlone, Matthew; Tofighbakhsh, Jessica (2000) *Birds of a Feather Flock Conjointly (?): Rhyme as Reason in Aphorisms*. https://journals.sagepub.com/doi/10.1111/1467-9280.00282 (accessed 2 November 2020).

Moran, Joe (2019) *First You Write a Sentence*. Penguin Random House.

Nahai, Nathalie (2012) *Webs of Influence: The Psychology of Online Persuasion*. Pearson.

Norman, Donald (2013) *The Design of Everyday Things*. Basic Books.

Oliver, Mary (1994) *Dream Work*. Atlantic Monthly Press.

Oppenheimer, Daniel M (2005) *Consequences of Erudite Vernacular Utilized Irrespective of Necessity: Problems with Using Long Words Needlessly*. https://onlinelibrary.wiley.com/doi/abs/10.1002/acp.1178 (accessed 2 November 2020).

Owen, Adrian, Dr (2018) *Into the Grey Zone*. Scribner Book Company.

Pinker, Steven (2008) *The Stuff of Thought*. Penguin.

Pinker, Steven (2015) *The Sense of Style*. Penguin Random House.

Redish, Ginny (2012) *Letting Go of the Words: Writing Web Content that Works*. Morgan Kaufmann.

Ritchie, Harry (2014) *English for the Natives: Discover the Grammar You Don't Know You Know*. John Murray.

Schriver, Karen A (1996) *Dynamics in Document Design*. Wiley.

Song, Hyunjin; Schwarz, Norbert (2009) *If It's Difficult to Pronounce, It Must Be Risky*. https://journals.sagepub.com/doi/abs/10.1111/j.1467-9280.2009.02267.x (accessed 2 November 2020).

Trask, RL (1997) *The Penguin Guide to Punctuation*. Penguin.

Williams, Joseph M; Bizup, Joseph (2016) *Style: Lessons in Clarity and Grace*. Pearson.

Wydick, Richard C; Sloan, Amy E (2019) *Plain English for Lawyers*. Carolina Academic Press.

INDEX